Twelve Scriptures That Saved My Life

Paul Volk

ISBN-10:0692785353
ISBN-13:9780692785355

To everyone who has been an example to me of life lived true. I count myself amazingly rich to know so many, too many to name on one page.

CONTENTS

GOD: LIKE ONE OF US

For there is one God, and one mediator also between God and men, the man Christ Jesus, 1 Timothy 2:5

There is a song from back a few decades that made it onto the radio and actually achieved some modest popularity. It was titled "One of Us."[1] It began, "What if God was one of us; just a slob like one of us, just a stranger on the bus trying to make his way home?" The language is about as unreligious as it gets. Are you offended by "a slob like one of us"? Is that any way to talk about God? That is not the way the incarnation is depicted in sermons and books on Christian theology. But that song is a much better, and much more helpful way of depicting the incarnation than what we typically hear on a Sunday morning.

---

[1] "One of Us,"Joan Osborn

Blue Gorilla Records, Mercury label, Feb. 21, 1995

From the album, "Relish"

The incarnation is by its very nature a shocking, offensive, messy and unreligious fact. And so it must be, because we humans are by our nature very shocking, offensive, messy and not all that spiritual. And we don't like to see that about ourselves. And so we have done with the incarnation what religious people always have done with biblical truth; we have cleaned it up, turned it into a piece of theology to be analyzed, studied and debated. And when we do that it loses its power to save our lives. Because when we become followers of Jesus of Nazareth we do not become bloodless, plaster saints. We still sometimes dribble saliva on our pillows when asleep. We are still, despite graduate degrees and beautiful suburban church buildings, more like slobs, still like strangers on a bus trying to make our way back home.

The Son of God, the spiritual, immaterial, eternal Son of God, the Word of God, became a real human being, just like us. And what is true of the living Word is true of the written Word; it is incarnate. The whole Bible is itself one long incarnation. It is the thoughts of eternal, immaterial God fully dwelling in sentences and paragraphs. It is filled with the very real lives of very human men and women in and through whom spiritual, theological truth is made incarnate, touchable, real to us in a way that mere theological and doctrinal truth cannot be. I have a great love for theology and doctrine. I do not want to in any way minimize their value. I also value maps. I depend on maps to get to places, especially places I have never been to before. But the map, no matter how well drawn, is not my destination. Alongside a map, I value a picture, a color, three dimensional picture, and better still a moving picture of my destination.

I have a great appreciation for and deeply value the human skeleton, the remarkable structure of bones in my body that keep it together, that enable me to walk and sit and live in this body. But that skeleton is there to support all the soft tissue, all the internal organs and blood and lymph and muscles and skin that make me what and who I am. It is hard to hug, or love a skeleton. If you want to see theological truth, to see the doctrine of incarnation, you need to see it incarnated, clothed in flesh and blood.

Walking skeletons are a mainstay of Halloween. They are images evoking horror and fear. Why is that? They are like Zombies, the walking dead. They frighten and repel us. Skeletons without flesh and blood and muscle are like truths without living, real human beings to embody them. Jesus, the man Jesus of Nazareth, said, "I am the truth." Truth is first a person, then verbal formulation. He is the living truth that sets men free. *For there is one God, and one mediator also between God and men, the man Christ Jesus…*[2] Truth incarnate, truth we can see and touch, truth become as human as we are saves us and sets us free.

There are a number of passages in the Bible which, at critical times, have saved my life. My faith was in danger of being swept away by doubt and profound disillusionment. What I needed was more than to hear faith explained; I needed to see faith incarnate, to see it

---

[2] 1 Timothy 2:5

being lived in a fully real, fully credible human being, in a "slob" like myself. Believing a proposition to be true is critical and powerful. But it is not the same as believing a person to be true. I needed to see faith incarnated in real, believable humanity. There is still only one mediator between me and God, the MAN Jesus, the Messiah.

More than half of the Bible is narrative. More than half of the Bible is a story. Reading the Bible is more like watching a play than taking a class in theology. A good play draws you in. A good play, with believable characters with whom you can identify, erases the distance between you and what is happening on the stage. You leave behind your assumed role of theater critic. A good play is the mediator between you and the author. A good play is the invisible author communicating with his or her audience. God's true story is written in flesh and blood. That is what I have come to experience and understand, first in Jesus himself and now in the written Word as well. I offer a record of some of my encounters with this written, incarnate, fully believable Word in hope that it will in some measure serve your faith and save your life as it has saved mine.

A HARD SAYING: John Chapter Six

So Jesus said to them, "Truly, truly, I say to you, unless you eat the flesh of the Son of man and drink his blood, you have no life in you... Many of his disciples, when they heard it, said, "This is a hard saying; who can listen to it?" (literally, "hearing, who can hear it?") But Jesus, knowing in himself that his disciples murmured at it, said to them, "Do you take offense at this? After this many of his disciples drew back and no longer went about with him. Jesus said to the twelve, "Do you also wish to go away?" Simon Peter answered him, "Lord, to whom shall we go? You have the words of eternal life; and we have believed, and have come to know, that you are the Holy One of God." [3]

Jesus was attracting a large following. Far from the nearest supermarket and fast food restaurant thousands of people had gathered to hear him. He turned a few fish and loaves of bread into enough food to feed them all. That's a very good way to multiply disciples and keep the attention of people.

He refers to Moses feeding the Israelites manna in the wilderness. They get it. The analogy is obvious to this Jewish audience. Israel had Moses in the wilderness. Israel had a cloud by day and a pillar of fire by night. That was all necessary. But how far

---

[3] John 6:53, 60-61, 66-69 RSV

would they get without bread to eat and water to drink? John identifies those present as disciples. They had witnessed the miracle of the bread and the fish. More than that, they had eaten some of the bread and the fish. He tells them that the bread that Moses gave to Israel was not the true bread. The true bread was his body. And the true drink was his blood. And unless they ate his body and drank his blood they had no life in them. These disciples *all* said, ""This is a hard saying; who can listen to it?" The literal Greek says, "Hearing, who can hear this?" (RSV John 6:60)

Those listening were all followers, all disciples. Among them was the inner circle of the twelve. John says "As a result of this many of His disciples withdrew and were not walking with Him anymore." (v. 66, NAU) And Jesus let them go. He did nothing to stop them. Now he turns to the twelve and asks, "Do you also want to go away?" (NKJV John 6:67)

It is dangerously easy, more than nineteen centuries later, to miss the enormity of the offensiveness of what Jesus had said. "… eat my flesh… drink my blood…" It was enough to cause many disciples to leave, to no longer follow him. And it is easy to miss the fact that Jesus did nothing… *nothing* to stop them. He let them go. Those who did not leave watched the others, the many, leave. And it wasn't until the next day, in the Capernaum synagogue, that he asked those who were still with him if they also wanted to leave. He gave them what must have been a very long and restless night to ponder what they had heard and seen the day before.

I had read that passage many times. But a time came when I heard it. A time came that caught me by surprise, when I found myself there in the synagogue. I was no longer in the audience watching the scene played out on the stage; this time I was on the stage and Jesus was asking me if I also wanted to go away. That's how you know that you have really heard what you have just read. The distance in time and space and culture and tradition is erased and you are right there. Cool detachment has just been evaporated away. Jesus has just turned to you and asked, "What about YOU? Are you offended? Do you want to leave too? Well, do you?"

I had heard him say some perplexing things. But now he was saying something more than perplexing. This was a hard saying, an offensive saying. It collided head on with a core understanding of the scriptures and Jewish religious practice. And as I stood there before him this hard saying brought fully into consciousness all the hard sayings that had been accumulating in my mind over many years. Only now they could not be filed away for future reference. The Lord had just asked me if what I heard made me want to leave. He was waiting for my answer and was not going to walk away and change the subject, or let me change the subject, until I answered.

"Hearing, who can hear this?" To the Jewish audience at that time there were few things more offensive that Jesus could have said. It was offensive enough to cause many disciples to turn and call it quits. And then Jesus said to those who remained, "What about you?" I was caught by surprise. I had come to think that being a believer, a disciple, meant never being offended by anything in the Bible. I had, more than I had realized, suppressed offense and bewilderment over words and events in the Bible. I probably would have continued to push them aside. Now I couldn't pretend they weren't there. Now I couldn't tell myself they didn't really mean what they seemed to mean. It was Jesus himself forcing me to face this and all the hard sayings. And they are hard sayings, hard, almost impossibly hard to hear. Now there was no "un-hearing." The cards lay open, face up on the table. And Jesus, the dealer, was asking me what I wanted to do. Do I want to fold them and get up from the table and walk away? This was not the hand I expected or ever wanted to play.

The Bible contains some sayings harder to hear than "eat my flesh and drink my blood." And they have caused many disciples who had followed Jesus for a long time to say "This is a hard saying; who can bear to hear it." True, he did finally explain that he did not mean actually eating his body and drinking his blood. But then why did he say it? Why did he wait for several thousand disciples to leave their cards on the table and get up and go home before he explained what he meant? And there are several other things recorded in the Bible, even harder to comprehend, that are not explained a few verses, or a thousand verses later. Life, both as recorded in scripture and on the evening news, is full of "hard sayings" which crash against and batter our understanding of God. Life, like scripture, brings not just a wave that is hard to stand in, one that challenges your ability to maintain your balance, but a natural and spiritual tsunami. "What about you, do you want to leave too?" What would the disciples answer? What would I answer?

Jesus wasn't asking me if I agreed with a biblical doctrine. He was asking me if I was going to stay or leave. Would I continue on with him or part company. A lot – everything – depended on the disciples' answer, on my answer. I imagined what I thought was the right religious response. I had come to expect the "right" religious answer from a disciple. So before continuing to read I began to mentally fill in the blank space after Jesus' question.

"Leave? Why would we leave? A genuine disciple would never be offended by anything you might say, by anything in all of the Bible. Isn't that what shows that we are genuine disciples? The fact that they left must mean that they had never been real disciples. We are, evidenced by the fact that we are still here, unoffended. Eat your flesh and drink your blood? No, we have no problem with that. We aren't offended by that."

Really? Well, how about some other "hard sayings?" How about Samuel the prophet coming to Saul and telling him that God is commanding him to go and kill all of the Amalekites? Go kill the Amalekites, the men, women, children, and infants, because of what their long dead ancestors did when they picked off the weak and the stragglers among our long dead ancestors on their way to Canaan.[4] After all, they have always opposed the people of God.

---

[4] 1 Samuel 15

I had read that passage a number of times before. And when you continue reading you never get to hear Samuel explain that no, of course he didn't mean literally kill all the children and babies. Because that is precisely what he did mean. I had read all this before. Only this time I found myself on the stage, in the play, standing beside Saul. This time I was not in a seminary class or a church Bible study. The relevant question now was not about how well I understood the biblical doctrine of Divine judgment. Now I was right there as Samuel turned to me and asked, "What about you? Are you offended? Will you go and draw your sword? Will you thrust your sword through the belly of the Amalekite baby crying on the ground beside its dead mother?" Or didn't you realize that this is what Samuel, and the God who sent him, was asking of YOU?

What should a genuine disciple respond? The choices seem to be clear and simple: obey or don't obey; stay or walk away; follow or call it quits. And isn't staying or leaving what reveals the genuineness or falsity of your discipleship? You are face to face with Samuel. You are standing over an infant with a sword in your hand. He is waiting for your response. This time you can't go home to read another commentary. You can't tell him you'll send him an email next week. He's waiting for your answer and he's not leaving until you give it. You weren't expecting this. You were simply having your "quiet time," reading through the Old Testament, your morning coffee on the table beside you. These are not the cards you thought you were being dealt. How are you going to play them? Are you in or are you out?

Oh. So this is not just a graphic Old Testament picture of how we are supposed to treat our sins when they appear in their most innocent, infant-like form. Oh. This is talking about something that really happened. Real men, with real swords in their hands, stood before real infants. Now I'm standing there with a sword in my hand. Now I'm being asked, not a doctrinal, theological, or exegetical question. Now I'm being asked what I am going to do with that sword. Until you realize that is what you are being asked you haven't really heard what the Bible is saying. Many disciples have stopped following Jesus when they heard Samuel's words, God's words, these words.

I have heard the response of many disciples, followers of Jesus, to Samuel's words and Saul's. In classrooms and living rooms and church Bible studies I have heard, rarely as clearly, but always in effect something like this:

"We have no problem with that. No, if we were there we would not have hesitated or thought twice about thrusting a sword into the bellies of children and infants. And wipe out the Canaanites? And the Holocaust...? We have no problem with that. We have learned all the "correct" biblical explanations. The tsunami that killed a few hundred thousand people in a few minutes? And Hell, a vast multitude of feeling, sentient human spirits experiencing unimaginable torment and agony for all eternity? No, we have no problem with that. They are just getting what they asked for, what they deserve. We have all the "correct" theological explanations. We have well prepared answers ready to give all who ask the questions. We have no questions, no doubts, no inner turmoil and anguish over that. Why would we want to call it quits and leave?"

Well, there are "correct" theological answers. But they are shallow and not fully understood until you are standing over a crying infant or walking through the wake of an Indian Ocean tsunami or talking to a Holocaust survivor. You haven't really heard the correct theological answer until you have to speak it and hear it coming out of your own mouth while standing face to face with reality. Now, for the first time, I was standing beside Peter and all the remaining disciples and Jesus was looking me in the face asking, "What about you? Do you want to leave also?" So I stopped and put the book aside before listening to Peter's answer. Now it mattered, really mattered, how he would respond.

My innermost thoughts were completely exposed. I had said, along with Peter and the other disciples, "Hearing this, who can hear it?" I was offended; my whole understanding of justice and compassion was offended, was exceeded. And I wanted to leave. What would Peter answer? If he said, "Leave? No way. Why would I want to leave? I'm your disciple. Nothing you could do or say would offend me," I would get up and walk away. I may have thought that would have been my answer before, but not now, not ever again. Now, to not be offended and perplexed would be a sign not of true discipleship but of religious insanity and betrayal of all truth and reality. No problem with what you said? I have a problem, a big problem, a staggering problem.

But if Peter didn't say he had no problem, what alternative was there? If he said "Yes, I want to leave also, we are all leaving," how could I then stay? So I waited. And there was no going back. I had heard. I was there.

What Jesus' question in Capernaum did was blow the religious, "correct" cover off of my "correct" answers and leave me exposed before him. Now the expected, the theologically "correct" answers turned to dry dust and were swept, not back under the carpet but right out the open front door.

I have struggled and gagged and choked on the hard sayings of Scripture and of life, especially over Scripture, over the hard sayings that come out of the mouth of God. I find it hard to imagine how anyone could NOT have a problem, could NOT find some of the sayings of the Bible hard and unbearable to hear. Now far more was at stake than the conclusion of a living room Bible study on the sixth chapter of John's gospel. Now whether or not I would be following Jesus tomorrow was on the line.

Then I looked back down and read, and heard what the disciples who remained said. They were still there. They hadn't left with the hundreds, or thousands who had. Why were they still there? What was keeping them? What was keeping me? It wasn't the "correct" religious answers. Those answers were sure to drive me away. Those answers were more offensive than the hard sayings to which they responded. I listened to hear what these disciples would say. They too found it hard, very hard to hear some of what Jesus the Lord, the Son of God, had said. But they were still there.

Simon Peter answered, *"Lord, to whom shall we go? You have the words of eternal life."* (v. 68)

I was stunned. Peter's answer became my own and it expanded, it elaborated in my mind. I stood beside Peter and I responded: "Lord, I have nowhere to go. There is nowhere else to go. I cannot spit out the hard, unpalatable words of yours because I understand that if I spit out the hard words, the words of life go out with them. Harder to eat than your literal flesh and blood are some of your words. You are telling me I must eat them all, I must take them into the innermost parts of my being, or I will have no life in me. I will keep seeking the understanding that will make them digestible. But if I have to carry the hard words like an indigestible lump in my spiritual gut until I die and stand before you, alright. Spitting them out is not an option. I don't have the option of picking and choosing from among your words on the basis of what I find digestible and agreeable. As you said, your words, even the most bitter ones, are true bread, and man lives by EVERY word that proceeds from the mouth of God. No, I'm not leaving. I know you. I don't always understand you, but I know you. You have the words that raised me from the dead, the words of eternal life. I can't leave. I won't leave."

There is no indication that those who remained ceased to find Jesus' words to be a hard saying. And Jesus never reproved them for having said that they were hard, very hard to hear. Yes, I know; he went on to tell them that flesh and blood doesn't profit them, that the words that he speaks are spirit and life. That helps, but doesn't answer the real question. What words of yours are spirit and life? The words Samuel spoke to Saul? The words you spoke about hell? The words about wiping out the Canaanites? You said some things very hard to hear and that ALL of them are spirit and life, all of them have to be eaten.

Peter spoke for all the disciples. Peter spoke for me. He said this was a hard saying. He didn't put a spiritual gloss over it. He gave the only reason for not leaving that I could honestly give and live with. "You have the words of eternal life. There is no where else to go." And that is why that passage saved my life. That is why I continued to believe and follow him. "Do you want to leave also?" The impulse to close the book and walk away has been very real at times in my Christian life. Redefining and rationalizing the hard sayings has been a temptation, but in the end never a real option. That day in the synagogue in Capernaum I understood what being a follower of Jesus really meant. It did not mean or require pretending to find every saying of Scripture palatable. It rested on seeing and believing that he has the words of eternal life, words that I have eaten, that have entered into the deeps of my soul and transformed me. And so there is nowhere else to go. I don't always understand him. I only know him.

I WOULD FLY AWAY: David, Psalm 55, Psalm 11

Give ear to my prayer, O God; And do not hide Yourself from my supplication.

Give heed to me and answer me; I am restless in my complaint and am surely distracted, Because of the voice of the enemy, Because of the pressure of the wicked; For they bring down trouble upon me And in anger they bear a grudge against me. My heart is in anguish within me, And the terrors of death have fallen upon me. Fear and trembling come upon me, And horror has overwhelmed me.

I said, "Oh, that I had wings like a dove! *I would fly away and be at rest. Behold, I would wander far away, I would lodge in the wilderness. I would hasten to my place of refuge from the stormy wind and tempest."[5]*

If David was alive and writing his Psalms today he would have a hard time finding a Christian publisher, at least within a certain segment of the Church world. If he prayed like he did in this Psalm he might be rebuked for his lack of faith. I mean, does God hide

---

[5] Psalm 55:1-9

himself from my supplication? And if I ever feel that he does, could I, should I ever give voice to what I am feeling? And what about "my heart is in anguish within me"? Is that the way any genuine, believing, God-trusting person could ever feel? Fear and trembling… overwhelmed with horror… how did those lines ever get past the angelic censor? Do they ever get past my "spiritual" inner censor?

I have spent more time more consistently in the Psalms than anywhere else in the Bible. They give voice to what I know and feel and what I am. They are honest and true and liberating. Jesus asked his faithful disciples if they wanted to go away. He didn't have to ask David. The horror and anguish were great enough, the fear and darkness crushing enough for him to say, *""Oh, that I had wings like a dove! I would fly away and be at rest. "Behold, I would wander far away, I would lodge in the wilderness. I would hasten to my place of refuge from the stormy wind and tempest."*

Do I want to leave too? Yes, sometimes I want to fly away. I want to find a quiet refuge away from the strife and confusion that I find not just in the world but in the Church, in the Bible, and most of all in my own soul. Oh, that I had wings like a dove! It is so wearying, so exhausting, so futile to keep telling myself and others that I never feel like escaping all the pressure of life. And it is deceitful. It is a lie spoken and believed in the name of faith. That's the evil of it. Being what we think is "spiritual" and "full of faith" turns us into liars and hypocrites. Then we are confronted by David.

We come into the prayer meeting in the church basement and there he is. "Hey, brother David! How's it going?" And we know what we expect to hear. Maybe he will say "O, not so good," and share some things that are troubling him. That much honesty we have pre-programmed ourselves to hear. But instead we hear "anguish... horror... O, that I had wings like a dove!" Nothing has prepared us for this. We are caught by surprise. What are you going to say to Brother David? How are you going to pray for him?

I have had times in my life as a believing disciple when the inner horror, the anguish and anxiety and fear finally overflowed the religious and spiritual banks and flooded my soul. And God seemed far away. And what I wanted most were wings, not to ascend to heaven but to fly away, to desert, to leave the front lines of unceasing war that is life in the world and stop fighting, and be just left alone. How could I ever feel that way, let alone give voice to those feelings? To whom could I say it? Who could hear it without repeating some memorized scripture, not because he knew it was what I needed to hear but because he had nothing else to say.

What I needed to hear at those times, what had to be said before I could hear anything else, was David. Ah, you too, David, man after God's own heart, father of the Lord that I trust and follow. What strange comfort it is to hear you in your anguish and horror. And I am so grateful to you. You have unlocked the vault of my soul and opened the way for me to cry out, "O, that I had the wings of a dove! I would fly away!"

Through David God gave me permission to wail and rage, to lament and fear and wish to fly away. He even gave me the words by which to say it. So, Lord Jesus, you really are a man, a man acquainted with sorrow and grief. You knew where to find the words to express all that you felt while hanging, nailed to a cross. "My God, My God, why have you forsaken me?"[6] David supplied the words for you, surely I could do no better. How else could you, or David, lift me out of my sorrow and grief but by knowing them yourself?

What David knew and spoke is a horror well beyond the "normal," the expected, the containable horror and anguish that we all meet in life. He put in words what happens when the flood water continues to rise, when it reaches the house top to which you have fled, and keeps rising. There are no easy answers to fall back on here. This Psalm saved my life. It brought that unbearable, that inconsolable, that unanswerable experience of horror and fear into the realm of the real lived life of a disciple, of a believer, of a man after God's own heart, of the incarnate son of God. It saved my life.

Psalm Eleven

The same David who wrote Psalm Fifty-five wrote Psalm Eleven.

---

[6] Psalm 22

"In the LORD I take refuge; How can you say to my soul, "Flee as a bird to your mountain; For, behold, the wicked bend the bow, They make ready their arrow upon the string To shoot in darkness at the upright in heart. If the foundations are destroyed, What can the righteous do?"

For the LORD is righteous, He loves righteousness; The upright will behold His face. [7]

"How can you say to my soul, flee as a bird to your mountain...?"

Without Psalm Fifty-five Psalm Eleven would ring hollow to me. David, you said you wanted wings to fly away. You were overwhelmed with horror. You wanted to escape, to go A.W.O.L. and leave the battle behind. The same man wrote, the same man lived both Psalms. That is what has saved me. That is what has secured my soul and deepened my trust and my faith. Because when I put these two Psalms together I see and understand what I have known without knowing, without being able to express. We are a deep and great paradox. From the same deep heart come "O, that I had wings like a dove..." and "How can you say to my soul, "Flee *as* a bird to your mountain..." Out of the deeps of my own soul proceed, ""Behold, I would wander far away, I would lodge in the wilderness. I would hasten to my place of refuge from the stormy wind and tempest." and "In the LORD I take refuge; How can you say to my

---

[7] Psalm 11:1-3,7

soul, "Flee *as* a bird to your mountain…"

David, your flight, your horror, the overwhelming of your soul did not, does not negate and belie your faith and trust in God as your refuge. You can both anguish in his felt absence and repose in his presence. You can say "I would fly away" but when you hear, "fly away" you respond, "How can you say to me fly away… God is my refuge." Finding rest in that paradox, in the real condition of my frail yet indestructible soul, is what has saved my life. It is what has enabled me to endure in the horror and the fear and the anguish. Seeing it, seeing the man of Psalm Fifty-five and the man of Psalm Eleven at the same time, as the same man, has saved my life.

The horror, the anguish is very deep. It needs to be reached and exposed. Because if it is not, then we can't discover, un-cover what lies deeper still, the peace and confidence that is greater.

GETHSEMENE Matt. 26

Then Jesus came with them to a place called Gethsemane, and said to His disciples, "Sit here while I go over there and pray." And He took with Him Peter and the two sons of Zebedee, and began to be grieved and distressed. Then He said to them, "My soul is deeply grieved, to the point of death; remain here and keep watch with Me." [8] Matthew 26:36-38

NKJV Matthew 26:38 Then He said to them, "My soul is exceedingly sorrowful, even to death. Stay here and watch with Me."

Jesus had chosen twelve men to be his inner circle of disciples. There was a larger circle of about seventy. I wonder how they felt, knowing that there were twelve who had so much greater access to the master, so much more intimate a knowledge of the Messiah. But even within the circle of twelve there was no semblance of modern egalitarianism. Twice Jesus drew three men aside, Peter, James and John. Both times they witnessed an extraordinary revelation. The other nine were not included.

---

[8] Matthew 26:36-38

The Bible does not present a picture of equal privilege. The equality seen among the disciples, even the inner circle, is an equality of human frailty and weakness and failure. Who are these privileged three disciples? John and James are the one's who asked to be seated on the right and left hand of Jesus when he comes in glory and takes his place on the royal throne. And Peter? Who do the gospels have boasting that he will never deny the Lord, that he is ready to go to prison and death with him? And all the disciples discussed among themselves who was the greatest.

The inequality of treatment within the circle of twelve is itself bound to disturb and offend any egalitarian notions that we moderns might bring to Scripture and our understanding of God and his unique Son. But that is not what saved my life. It is what Peter and John and James saw that did.

The first time Jesus drew these three apart was when he brought them up to the top of a mountain with him. What they saw there was the momentarily unveiled glory of God. On the top of the mountain they saw Jesus unzip his flesh and let the inner, overwhelming reality of his divinity break out.

> *Six days later Jesus took with Him Peter and James and John his brother, and led them up on a high mountain by themselves. And He was transfigured before them; and His face shone like the sun, and His garments became as white as light. And behold, Moses and Elijah appeared to them, talking with Him. Peter said to Jesus, "Lord, it is good for us to be here; if You wish, I*

will make three tabernacles here, one for You, and one for Moses, and one for Elijah." While he was still speaking, a bright cloud overshadowed them, and behold, a voice out of the cloud said, "This is My beloved Son, with whom I am well-pleased; listen to Him!" When the disciples heard this, they fell face down to the ground and were terrified. And Jesus came to them and touched them and said, "Get up, and do not be afraid."[9]

Before going back down he told them not to talk to anyone about what they had experienced on the mountain top. Well, at some point, probably after Jesus' crucifixion and resurrection, they did tell about what they had seen and the account found its way into the Gospels. So why did Jesus bring them up to the mountain and let them see his unveiled glory? I think it has something to do with the conversation Peter, James and John overheard between Moses, Elijah and Jesus. They spoke of Jesus' soon coming departure, of his crucifixion. What these three saw on the mountain was essential to their understanding of what they would soon see in the garden.

That is not the only time he took these three aside to witness something extraordinary. It is what they saw in Gethsemane that has had a greater and more life and faith saving effect on me.

On the mount they saw his divinity. In the garden they saw his humanity. In both places they saw his glory.

---

[9] Matthew 17:1-7

They came to a place named Gethsemane; and He said to His disciples, "Sit here until I have prayed." And He took with Him Peter and James and John, and began to be very distressed and troubled.[10]

And being in agony He was praying very fervently; and His sweat became like drops of blood, falling down upon the ground.[11]

And He said to them, "My soul is deeply grieved to the point of death; remain here and keep watch."[12]

And He went a little beyond them, and fell to the ground and began to pray that if it were possible, the hour might pass Him by. And He was saying, "Abba! Father! All things are possible for You; remove this cup from Me; yet not what I will, but what You will."[13]

This is the gospel writers' description of Jesus, not while being crucified, not while hanging on the cross, but when looking just ahead, clearly seeing what he was about to suffer. Foreseeing and giving himself to the suffering of crucifixion was itself a supreme, an overwhelming agony and torture of his soul. This is his state of mind when he prays about the cup being given to him by his Father to drink, to be drained to the last drop of physical and mental torment and pain. And this is what saved my life and my faith. It is in full apprehension of what he was yielding himself to that he said to his omnipotent Father, *"If there is any way, let this cup pass from me."*

---

[10] Mark 14:32-33
[11] Luke 22:44
[12] Mark 14:34
[13] Mark 14:35

What does faith look like in the face of great suffering? How does a man or woman in whom the Spirit of God dwells, in whom and through whom the Messiah lives, approach pain and suffering and death? There are assurances in Scripture about an experience of grace that will bring us through all suffering. Well, how did the Son of God approach the greatest agony and suffering in his human body and mind?

How he did *not* pray has been very instructive and life-saving for me. He did *not* pray, "Father, if there is any way, make the cup bigger and fill it higher." His sonship did not exempt him from or diminish the very human response to terrible anguish and suffering.

I had been schooled in a kind of spirituality that exalted suffering. I was told that if a little suffering perfects a little, then a lot of suffering... you can fill in the blank. A lot of suffering perfects a lot. Granted, no one will or can face the depth and horror of suffering that Jesus went through. But the crucial point to realize is that his divinity did not reduce or alter the human response to pain and horror.

We have not understood Gethsemane until we are drawn out of the church basement or the living room Bible study or the morning "quiet time" reading of the Scriptures and transported across time and space to the dark night in the garden with Peter, James and John, just prior to the crucifixion. It is needful to see the Son of God in agony of soul, in deep inner wrestling, with the capillaries in his forehead bursting and blood dripping on the ground as he says to his

Father, "NEVERTHELESS... your will not mine be done." Never the less, despite apprehending the unedited, un-sanitized, un-retouched reality of extreme suffering; nevertheless, your will be done. "Your will, not mine be done" is said AFTER "If there is any way, let this cup pass from me."

How does a disciple pray in the face of great suffering? The answer is: like Jesus, the Son of God. Seeing him in the garden, hearing him pray, has set me free to pray without preconceived ideas of what spirituality sounds and looks like. A genuine disciple prays, "Father, IF THERE IS ANY WAY... let this cup pass from me." Jesus had no false "spiritual" vision of suffering. He wanted to live; he did not want to suffer. Jesus was human. His whole body and mind recoiled in horror and anguish at the prospect of the agony and pain he was about to endure. And he prayed, "LET THIS CUP PASS FROM ME. He was a man, a human being, and so am I. It is madness to think I could be, or should be, more "spiritual" than him when facing great, overwhelming horror and suffering.

It is only after responding as a man, responding truly, believably, that he said "Nevertheless..." What I understood was that faith resides not in reaching out for the cup but in the "nevertheless." Faith is not exhibited in the ease and peace with which I embrace pain and agony. Faith is not evidenced by some sublime, mystical indifference to torture and pain. Faith does not delete pain and torment from consciousness. It is not a spiritual narcotic. Faith is in the "nevertheless." I have been set free by what I saw in Gethsemane, free to pray like a man, like a human being with a real physical body, like Jesus prayed. He taught us how to pray not only in response to the disciples' request when he gave us the model of what is now referred to as the Lord 's Prayer. He taught us how to pray whenever he prayed. He taught us how to pray when he took Peter and James and John aside with him in the garden.

And I have been set free by seeing these three men overwhelmed, by seeing them shut down and lapse into sleep there in the garden. And what did we expect? They lapsed into foolish babble about building a tabernacle on the Mount of Transfiguration. What would be the human response to witnessing this later, greater transfiguration in the garden in the deep dark of night? We need to see the divinity of Jesus. We need to ascend the mount with him and be overwhelmed, and have our very meager grasp of his God-nature expanded beyond our grasp. And we need to see his humanity beyond the meager understanding we have been accustomed to. And that comes from finding ourselves in the garden at night seeing something we cannot bear to see.

The disciples heard something in the synagogue in Capernaum that, hearing, who could hear? They saw something on the mount that seeing, who could see? That is the hearing and seeing that transfigures us, that sets us free.

DO YOU BELIEVE IN THE RESURRECTION?
First Corinthians 15

I have been directly asked that question only once. It was not in a seminary class or a Bible study. It was at a time when my life had fallen apart. It was as if I had been riding on a wagon pulled by a team of horses. Before I was a Christian I had managed to control the horses well enough to stay on the road and get through some very difficult times. As a believer I was managing much better, but it was still true that those horses had a mind of their own. It took a very firm grip on the reins to keep the wagon from being pulled off the road. Then a crisis came along that made all that had come before it seem unworthy to be called crises. The reins fell out of my hands. I saw them down on the ground in front of me, under the horses' hooves. And the horses were racing ahead, out of control. My mind was out of control. All the fear and anxiety that I had always – sometimes just barely – been able to contain were now wildly racing, unrestrained. For the first time in my life I knew, I mean really knew, what it was to be out of control.

Sleep became almost impossible. I lost a lot of weight, and I hadn't started out with a surplus that I could afford to lose. I was falling apart, breaking down. I prayed very differently than I had when I still had the reins in my hands. My words to God were more earnest, more honest, less edited. I raged. "Where are you? Why is this going on without relenting and without your comfort? Don't you see? Don't you care? Help! Answer!" And there was no help and no comfort and no answer. Until one morning, when things were bad enough that I could see in my mind the local emergency room out in front of me, that I heard the voice of God.

I am always very skeptical when I hear people say "And God said... the Lord said to me..." My God has never been very loquacious. But this was one of those times when I, skeptic that I am, had no doubt. And what I heard was...

"Do you believe in the resurrection?"

My first reaction was not good. That's it? I have been bellowing at heaven for weeks, for months, feeling like my mind was one thread away from completely unraveling. I have pounded on your front door and no one answered. And now, when you do come, it is with... a theological question? Do I have to pass a pop quiz before you intervene and keep me from losing my mind? But as I sat there on my bedroom floor that question kept resonating. It was a stone dropped in the middle of a pond. The stone sank to the bottom and as it went down ripples began to spread out from where it had landed, little circular waves, until they filled the pond, until they reached and lapped the shore all around. And I understood. Oh, I believed in the resurrection. But there is a believing that changes everything. If I believed in the resurrection what would what I was passing through feel like? If I really believed, what would my state of mind be? What I knew for certain was that it wouldn't be what it presently was.

What I was tasting was death. It was the power of death to overcome life, to break down, disintegrate, neutralize all resistance. As long as death held the winning hand it really didn't matter what strategies you used against it. I didn't matter how skilled you were at playing the game or what cards you held. You would lose in the end. The doctrine of resurrection, the right theology, as long as that was all it was, was just one more card in your losing hand. But believing, knowing that the game had already been won, that a real man, Jesus of Nazareth had walked into death and come out the other side alive, and had taken you with him… that alone was enough to change everything.

And from that day on things began to turn. Like all the important, life saving lessons, this one came at great cost. But it was, looking back, worth it.

Paul devoted a significant amount of space to the resurrection in his letter to the believers in Corinth. He understood that it was no mere doctrine. He understood that there were no "mere doctrines."

And so he explained that if Jesus was not really resurrected from being really dead then there is no resurrection. And if there is no resurrection…. What? What if there is no resurrection, Paul? I paused. What would he say; how would he answer that question?

Once again a very pious, very religious answer came to my mind. "Live a good, sacrificial life, a good Christian life anyway." And when that occurred to me I recoiled. Paul, if that is your answer we will part company. Because it is a lie. If death is the end of all things, if death wins in the end, then all meaning, all purpose dies with it. If death is the ultimate black hole then it swallows up all hope, all light, all meaning. I came to understand death long before I understood life. It is the last and greatest enemy. The fear of death is the ultimate weapon in the devil's arsenal. Paul, don't give me some pious nonsense as an answer. If you do I will lose all trust in you. I don't care how finely argued your theology is. If there is no resurrection I don't care about the meaning of justification. If there is no resurrection I don't care what anyone says about sanctification. All I care about is getting through tomorrow without descending into a pit of depression, still able to enjoy a walk in the woods and the taste of a ripe strawberry.

And so with quickened pulse I read on. If there is no resurrection, "*If the dead are not raised, let us eat and drink, for tomorrow we die.*"[14] Or, in the words of Janis Joplin, "Get it while you can!" And what rose up in response in me was, "Yes!" Paul's words landed like

---

[14] 1 Corinthians 15:32

a wrecking ball on the edifice of false piety, false spirituality and mere religion. Thank you, Paul. Thank you for surprising candor, fully human honesty, truth and reality. You have won my trust. Everything depends on Jesus breaking out of the tomb, passing through and out of death never to die again. Believing that death has been conquered is right at the center of what salvation means. It is the wellspring of all faith and courage in the face of fear and depression and anxiety and dread.

Most to Be Pitied...? What if there is no resurrection? *"If we have hoped in Christ in this life only, we are of all men most to be pitied."*[15] What an odd answer. Why "Most to be pitied"? If Jesus stayed dead we won't know that until after we have died, and once we have died we won't know or care about anything. So why "Most to be pitied"? We will have lived with a great hope that transformed our lives. Isn't that enough? Isn't that a reason to be envied? But Paul said that belief in a lie is never to be envied. Belief in a lie, no matter how comforting and encouraging, makes us the greatest of fools, pitiful fools. We will have forfeit pleasures and endured rejection and ridicule for nothing. If my Christian faith, if ANYTHING, is for this passing, soon to be extinguished life only, then it is not something to be envied or admired. I am most to be pitied because I have lived a lie.

I love Paul. I love his love for truth. I love his dread and rejection of self-deception without regard to how good that self-

---

[15] 1 Corinthians 15:19

36

deception might make you feel. This is the same Paul who explained the reason for final damnation as not receiving a love for the truth so as to be saved.[16] This is the same Paul who wrote, *"But we should always give thanks to God for you, brethren beloved by the Lord, because God has chosen you from the beginning for salvation through* **sanctification by the Spirit and faith in the truth.**[17] Faith is not an end in itself. If you have faith my question is, "Faith in what?" If it is not faith in the truth I don't envy you; I pity you.

Jesus told a parable about a man who became very rich.

> *Then he said [to himself], "This is what I will do: I will tear down my barns and build larger ones, and there I will store all my grain and my goods. And I will say to my soul, soul, you have many goods laid up for many years to come; take your ease, eat, drink and be merry." But God said to him, "You fool! This very night your soul is required of you; and now who will own what you have prepared?" So is the man who stores up treasure for himself, and is not rich toward God.[18]*

"You fool!" Those are strong words, especially strong when spoken by God to a man. What made him a fool? Building a bigger barn, setting up an IRA and buying some gold coins is practical wisdom. Why is he called a fool? There is a resurrection. There is a final and all-defining confrontation with Reality, with Truth. Every

---

[16] 2 Thessalonians 2:10
[17] 2 Thessalonians 2:13
[18] Luke 12:18-21

scale of values will be fundamentally altered. Every present value and pleasure will be recast. How you see everything now is not reality. Therefore regarding it as reality is insane. Resurrection changes everything. *"Eat, drink, and be merry for tomorrow we die"*[19] is wisdom and sanity… if there is no resurrection.

Paul saved me from empty religion, from false spirituality, from a religiously warped view of what it means to be a human who lives in a physical body. Paul saved me from a deluded view of death as somehow normal and acceptable. He reminded me that it is not normal and not something to accept but something to hate and rage against. "Do you believe in resurrection?" I, like most of us, come to God seeking answers. I come to him with questions. And more times than not he responds not with an answer but with another question. "What about you, do you want to leave also?" "Do you believe in resurrection?" And the questions he asks prove to be better than any answer I was looking for. His questions have lead to answers I wasn't looking for. His questions have saved my life.

---

[19] Luke 12:19

A REAL CONVERSATION: Abraham and God, Genesis 18

If you stop and think about what a conversation is you will find yourself amazed. It is a form of intercourse, an exchange of the inner contents of the soul., mind to mind, heart to heart. We often talk without really listening. And we are constantly talking, if not to each other then internally, to and with ourselves. We are rightly told how important it is to be talking to God. There are very many books written about prayer. How to pray, what to pray, when to pray... and most if not every prayer recorded in Scripture has been analyzed, taught on and studied. What I find much more interesting are the conversations recorded in the Bible, the conversations between a human being and God. We talk about and write books about listening to God, recognizing the voice of God. Some of them are helpful. Some of them are not helpful at all. A lot of nonsense gets taught about hearing the voice of God. But as important as that is I find the actual conversations recorded in the Bible between God and man, between the Son of God and men and women, much more important and instructive. It is an astonishing thing to consider that God enters into real conversations with men and women. It is here that real relationship takes place. It is in real conversation that we discover and connect with each other. It is no different with God. One such conversation – between Abraham and God – ranks very high among the Bible passages that have changed, really saved my life.

The whole story of Abraham's life can be seen as an extended conversation with God. In the eighteenth chapter of Genesis the angel of the Lord, along with two angels, has come to judge and destroy the cities of Sodom and Gomorrah. On the way he has stopped for lunch with Abraham. Stopped for lunch? In earlier chapters the word of God had come to Abraham. And the Lord has appeared to Abraham in a vision. That fits well with our understanding and expectations about hearing from God. But lunch? Out in front of Abraham's tent? Eating and drinking with… God? That's what is going on in chapter eighteen and that is already revolutionary. Out in Abraham's front yard he is eating and drinking and conversing with God. Apparently God is not as concerned as we often are about how familiar, how accessible he lets himself be with human beings. The incarnation of the Son of God is the ultimate condescension, that is, the coming down of God to man. God understands that unless you are face to face, at eye-level, you can't have a real conversation.

When my daughter was little, about three or four or five years old, we often had guests in our house. I was very conscious of if and how they would respond to her. For some she appeared to not exist. For others she was unworthy of any attention. Most irritating to me were the ones who lapsed into the idiotic adult version of baby talk. It's the way waitresses sometimes talk to older, "senior" diners. It's embarrassing. It's demeaning. When someone paused to say hello to Stephanie, when someone knelt down to be face to face with her, I took note.

In one sense the Bible (and life) is one prolonged readjustment of our understanding of God, a continuous transformation of the relationship between man and God. And that relationship is eternal life. Jesus said that. He defined eternal life as knowing God and himself.[20] So getting to know the Father and his Son more truly, more as they really are, is not optional. It *is* eternal life. The conversation between Abraham and God after the angels depart for Sodom has transformed my understanding of God, my relationship with him. It has been a life-saving transformation.

> *The LORD said [to the two angels], "Shall I hide from Abraham what I am about to do, since Abraham will surely become a great and mighty nation, and in him all the nations of the earth will be blessed? For I have chosen him, so that he may command his children and his household after him to keep the way of the LORD*

---

[20] John 17:1-3

by doing righteousness and justice, so that the LORD may bring upon Abraham what He has spoken about him." [21]

I have to wonder what the angels thought when they heard this. I know what I might have thought. "Lord, you are God. You don't have to explain yourself to any man. He is made of dust. We are spirit like you and you owe us no explanations." Well, they are right, God owes us no explanations. God owes us nothing. Abraham has not asked why the Lord and two angels are walking down the road that passes his tent. It is God who asks, rhetorically, "Shall I hide what I am about to do from Abraham?" The answer is understood. No. I can't hide it from him. I chose him to father a great nation, the people in and through whom the Son of God is going to come into the world. I am God, far above man. I am God MOST HIGH. But I have a relationship with the son of Terah. I am going to tell him what I am about to do. I can't NOT tell him.

Lord, are you sure you want to do that? I have heard things in the Bible; I have heard words out of your mouth that hearing, I could not bear to hear. Almost all of them were about judgment. These are the hardest of the hard sayings. God knows what he is about to do. Sodom and Gomorrah are going to be buried in molten lava, burned with fire. Everyone is going to die, all the men, the women, and all the children. Or did you think there were no children and nursing babies in Sodom? And you have to tell Abraham what you are going to do? I read that and once again the pages in front of me opened up

---

[21] Genesis 18:17-19

and drew me in. I was standing there now on the road along with the two angels. I wanted to say to the Lord, you know what response you are going to get. He will either swallow hard and say nothing and pretend he didn't hear what you said, or... or what? It is God, not Abraham, who initiates what promises to be an unusual, a very difficult conversation.

I needed to see that. More than I realized I needed to see that. I had questions for God, questions about what he has done and what he said he will do. It is a fearful thing to question God. Coming in arrogance, coming as if from above him, coming to interrogate him is not something any man can safely do. But denying that we have questions, moral struggles with God, is no better; in fact it is bound to be worse than coming as his accuser. Still, who am I to question God? The answer is, I am a son of Abraham. I am a son of his faith, a son of his chosenness, an heir of the relationship that my father, Abraham, had with God. The way God related to Abraham, the kind of conversation they had together, the kind of conversation that God initiated and invited Abraham into is open to me. God is inviting me to question him. God has raised the questions in my mind, not me. Therefore I can, I have to, I am free to ask them.

That fact alone has radically, I mean radically, down to the roots, to the core, changed the way I know and relate to God. He actually believes that he should share with us, with me, what he intends to do. He has opened, and left open the door between himself and Abraham, between himself and me. That is astonishing. That goes against the understanding of God that too many of his people hold to. That demolishes an enormous barrier between him and me. But that is only the beginning. The actual conversation is even more astonishing and more transforming and revealing.

> *And the LORD said, "The outcry of Sodom and Gomorrah is indeed great, and their sin is exceedingly grave. "I will go down now, and see if they have done entirely according to its outcry, which has come to Me; and if not, I will know." Then the men turned away from there and went toward Sodom, while Abraham was still standing before the LORD. Abraham came near and said, "Will You indeed sweep away the righteous with the wicked?"* [22]

When the Lord said this Abraham was "still standing before the Lord." He heard every word. He heard God say that the sin of these cities was "exceedingly grave." The Lord is there, and the angels going on before him are there, to determine the full extent of the sin and evil of Sodom and Gomorrah. Abraham responds to what he has just heard with a question. He comes near. That little detail arrested my attention. How near to this God am I prepared to come, to ever come, and especially with the question I am about to ask? Because Abraham's question has long been my question. *"Will You indeed sweep away the righteous with the wicked?"*

Abraham, do you realize who you are talking to?

Abraham is a finite mortal. He does not share God's

---

[22] Genesis 18:20-23

omniscience. What he has just heard does not sound good. He knows who God is. And still, he asks this question. It is understandable. The judgment to come is vast and all encompassing. Flowing, molten lava is not selective. And at the same time the question is not understandable. Abraham, do you really think you need to ask that question? This is not a man you are talking to; it is God Most High, it is the Lord.

I heard a Bible teacher who I very highly esteem respond to a question about God judging whole Canaanite tribes and the Amalekites. He said God can kill whomever he chooses to kill. The implication upon which such a response rests is that God, simply because he is God, cannot be questioned. His justice cannot be questioned. If God had given a similar answer to Abraham I would have left. I would not still be here. But that was not God's answer.

> *"Suppose there are fifty righteous within the city; will You indeed sweep it away and not spare the place for the sake of the fifty righteous who are in it Far be it from You to do such a thing, to slay the righteous with the wicked, so that the righteous and the wicked are treated alike. Far be it from You! Shall not the Judge of all the earth deal justly?"* [23]

This sounds very much like Abraham is instructing God. *"Far be it from you!"* He says that twice… to God. *"Shall not the Judge of all the earth deal justly?"* How should God respond to such a question? Is it an expression of doubt and unbelief… or of faith? Is it arrogant

---

[23] Genesis 18:24-25

presumption or born out of humility? It is faith. He so trusted God that he could be completely candid, that he could speak out of his understanding of justice face to face with God. Abraham told God what God could not do. You are bound by justice, limited by your own just nature. If there are fifty righteous men you can't destroy the city! And God does not reprove Abraham. He does not tower over him and say, "Who do you think you are? You piece of dust, are you instructing me in righteousness? You who lied about your wife – twice – to save your own skin? You who took Hagar and got her pregnant? You, who along with Sarah, laughed in my face when I said next year you will have a son?"[24]

There is not one word of rebuke in this whole dialogue between God and Abraham. God lets this very imperfect, very fallible man question him. And Abraham goes on, pressing his argument further.

> *So the LORD said, "If I find in Sodom fifty righteous within the city, then I will spare the whole place on their account." And Abraham replied, "Now behold, I have ventured to speak to the Lord, although I am but dust and ashes. "Suppose the fifty righteous are lacking five, will You destroy the whole city because of five?" And He said, "I will not destroy it if I find forty-five there."* [25]

"I have ventured to speak to the Lord, although I am but dust and ashes."

---

[24] Genesis 17:17, 18:12
[25] Genesis 18:26-28

I have lived with pressing, almost crushing questions about the justice of some of God's judgments. Such questions do not dissolve away. But how do you ask the Most High God, the God who gave his only begotten Son, the God who created heaven and earth, the God who is a consuming fire, if he is being just? *"I have ventured to speak to the Lord, although I am but dust and ashes"* because it is God who said *"How can I not tell him what I am about to do?"* **God began this conversation**. I was invited in to this frank, this morally perilous, this fully exposed conversation. That is why this passage of scripture has saved my life. It has freed me to not only petition and praise and worship God but also to question him. It has shown me that faith can be expressed in questions born of perplexity. It has shown me that the God I know will not glower and fume at my apparent presumption but will hear me and answer because I am Abraham's son, because, with all of my frailty and sin, I am God's son.

Astonishingly, Abraham presses on.

> *He spoke to Him yet again and said, "Suppose forty are found there?" And He said, "I will not do it on account of the forty." Then he said, "Oh may the Lord not be angry, and I shall speak; suppose thirty are found there?" And He said, "I will not do it if I find thirty there." And he said, "Now behold, I have ventured to speak to the Lord; suppose twenty are found there?" And He said, "I will not destroy it on account of the twenty." Then he said, "Oh may the Lord not be angry, and I shall speak only this once; suppose ten are found there?" And He said, "I will not destroy it*

on account of the ten." As soon as He had finished speaking to Abraham the LORD departed, and Abraham returned to his place. [26]

My way of seeing and relating to God has been changed. And so has my way of seeing Abraham, and myself. My one lingering question as the chapter concludes is not for God but for Abraham. "Abraham, why did you stop at ten?" What if there was only one righteous man? Maybe he did not need to ask that last question. Maybe he left it for me to ask.

---

[26] Genesis 18:29-33

LET'S ARGUE IT OUT: Isaiah 1:18

Isaiah 1:18 *"Come now, and **let us reason together**," Says the LORD, "Though your sins are as scarlet, They will be as white as snow; Though they are red like crimson, They will be like wool.."*

NRS Isaiah 1:18 *"Come now, **let us argue it out**," says the LORD: "though your sins are like scarlet, they shall be like snow; though they are red like crimson, they shall become like wool."*

This verse had long intrigued me. "Let us reason together" seemed such a strange invitation. Then the NRS[27] translation drove it home, deep into my understanding. "Let's argue it out." Lord, I must have misheard you. What exactly are you saying? The word "argue" has mostly negative connotations. It evokes contention, conflict. But its meaning extends beyond the negative. Pursuing a logical conclusion is also referred to as an argument. That's why God's invitation to "argue it out" had so great an impact on me. I have often said that it is alright to argue with God, as long as you

---

[27] New Revised Standard version

desire (and expect) to lose the argument more than you desire (and expect) to win it. And, just as the only way to arrive at an answer is by first asking a question, the only way to reach a conclusion is to first make your case, to argue for it.

There are a few scriptures that seem to rule out arguing with God even though Abraham did just that, and so did Jacob, who I want to talk about later.

> *Seek the LORD while He may be found; Call upon Him while He is near. Let the wicked forsake his way and the unrighteous man his thoughts; And let him return to the LORD, And He will have compassion on him, And to our God, For He will abundantly pardon. "For My thoughts are not your thoughts, nor are your ways My ways," declares the LORD. "For as the heavens are higher than the earth, So are My ways higher than your ways And My thoughts than your thoughts.*[28]

This is not the only scripture that has been misunderstood and misapplied. It should be obvious that the Lord is not saying that we should abandon all thinking. It is the wicked who need to abandon their wicked, rebellious ways of thinking not the righteous who should sit silently, thoughtlessly, and nod. True, God's thoughts are not the same as ours. His ways are far above ours. But that does not mean that there is no overlap, no common meaning and understanding between us. Abraham's idea of justice was not so different from God's that they could not talk about it together. The

---

[28] Isaiah 55:6-9

Bible, all one thousand plus pages of it, is evidence that God thinks he can communicate with us using words that we can understand, if not fully and perfectly then sufficiently to arrive at a correct knowledge of him and of the Gospel, sufficiently to make it possible to have a real conversation.

> *Trust in the LORD with all your heart and do not lean on your own understanding. In all your ways acknowledge Him, And He will make your paths straight. Do not be wise in your own eyes; Fear the LORD and turn away from evil.*[29]

If you do acknowledge God in all your ways and don't think you are wiser and smarter than you are, or than he is, where does that leave you? The point of the proverb is: don't lean on or rely on your own understanding above all things, including God. The point is not to abandon and disregard your mind and your limited understanding. Turn away, not from your mind and thoughts but from evil and an unwarranted, inflated estimation of them.

There are too many calls in Scripture, both in the Old and New Testaments, to seek understanding to ever conclude that we should not use our minds to the full.[30]

The passage in Isaiah is another invitation to "argue it out" with God. He is not afraid of or put off by a good, sincere argument or disagreement. *Iron sharpens iron, So one man sharpens another.*[31] That

---

[29] Proverbs 3:5-7
[30] The words "understand" and "understanding" occur in 256 verses in the Bible.
[31] Proverbs 27:17

applies to God sharpening man when he comes down and invites us to make our case with him. And when iron sharpens iron, sometimes sparks fly. That is to be expected. It's not a sign of something gone wrong.

Is it alright to argue with God? It is essential to argue with him as long as you come with humility and remain fully cognizant of who it is you are arguing with. And it is impolite to not accept his invitation. He is the one who said, "Come..." Remember, he sought out Abraham, not the other way around. That meant there was a way of making one's case that was not an expression of pride or contention but actually an expression of faith. Many of my agreements with God began in disagreement. I trusted him enough to be real and honest with him. That has been liberating. That has saved my life.

JACOB WRESTLING WITH GOD: GEN. 32

Jacob has lived far from home for close to twenty years. He left in flight from his angry brother, Esau. He left in fear. Now he is about to cross the Kidron brook and on the other side is Esau. Time has not erased Jacob's deception and fraud of twenty years ago. Time never does. He is alone at night. And he is afraid of what awaits him in the morning. And so he prays. He prays fervently that the God of his fathers will bless him, will be with him, alongside him, when he stands face to face with his brother, Esau. I have heard it said that God always hears and answers our prayers, just not always in the way we want or expect. I am very sure that what happened that night is not what Jacob expected.

I can identify with Jacob, both in his being alone in the dark, and in his fear. What has happened during dark, fear-filled nights in my life has not been what I expected. I asked for divine intervention, for a miraculous deliverance, and received instead a theological question. Jacob prayed for help from the God who had promised to bring him back alive and well to the land he fled from. Instead he looked up and saw a man.

Then Jacob was left alone, and a man wrestled with him until daybreak. Gen. 32:24

If not immediately, then very soon, Jacob understood that this was no ordinary man. No mere man could bless Jacob. No mere man could impart the strength and courage to face Esau. The Scripture simply says that this man wrestled with Jacob all night. Nothing is said about what, if any conversation took place. Nor are we told how the wrestling match started. Did Jacob grab hold of the man? Did this man begin to wrestle with Jacob? The context suggests that Jacob, desperate for a "blessing," grabbed hold and would not let go.

I'm not a fighter. I have known intense fear but fear is more likely to arouse my inner coward than my inner wrestler. It takes desperation for me to push the cowardly me aside. I have been instructed and encouraged by Jacob. He knew with whom he was wrestling. Now what? Jacob, a man, a very imperfect man, grabbing hold of... God; not just reaching out and touching but wrestling with... God? This is several steps beyond a polite conversation.

But more astonishing than Jacob grabbing hold of God is God wrestling with Jacob. Jacob took hold and did not, would not let go. Alright, I get it. I've heard numerous sermons and admonitions to persevere in prayer, to knock and keep on knocking. But now the graphics have changed. Now I am not picturing myself alone in my room or on the beach, or beside the Kidron, persevering in prayer through the fear-filled night. Now I am seeing two men, not frail, fearful Jacob alone. Jacob is wrestling with God. *And God is wrestling with Jacob.*

Once again I was no longer in the audience watching but up on the stage, right beside the brook, in the dark, the dusty desert ground beneath my feet. God was down in the dirt with Jacob, God was rolling in the dirt with this heel grabbing schemer. And Jacob would not let go. Neither would God. God, you could have ended this after one hour, or one minute, or one second. This is not exactly an even match. The outcome was never in doubt. And you had your promises to Jacob well in mind. You don't forget or renegotiate your promises. You knew from the beginning that you would bless Jacob. So why "all night"? I understand the need for Jacob to persevere. But you weren't simply out of sight and silent. You were down in the dirt with him. You held yourself back so that he could let himself go all out.

When he saw that he had not prevailed against him, he touched the socket of his thigh; so the socket of Jacob's thigh was dislocated while he wrestled with him. Then he said, "Let me go, for the dawn is breaking." But he said, "I will not let you go unless you bless me." [32]

How did it end? God saw that he had not prevailed against him. Jacob didn't win the match. He didn't pin God to the ground. No angelic referee was there to count to three. Jacob fought to a draw. You can't expect to win an argument with God. But apparently you can wrestle him to a draw. That doesn't mean that Jacob proved to

---

[32] Genesis 32:25-26

be too strong for God. The match has reached its necessary conclusion. Jacob, the mere man, was not going to let go. The sun was coming up. The night was ending. And God touched Jacob in the socket of his thigh. That is perilously close to the center of his manhood, his human strength. "Touched," all it took was a touch and Jacob was finished. His hip was dislocated. And he still would not let go.

So he said to him, "What is your name?" And he said, "Jacob." He said, "Your name shall no longer be Jacob, but Israel; for you have striven with God and with men and have prevailed." Genesis 32:27-28

Wait a minute. Jacob has prevailed? You just crippled him. How did he prevail? It must be simply by not giving up. This is where God changes Jacob's name. The usurper, the heal-grabbing schemer has his name changed to Mighty with God. It is after a night of wrestling that Jacob becomes Israel. He is crippled. He will be limping in the morning when he faces Esau. And every day after that. Some blessing. God blesses Jacob by crippling him. God rewards his prevailing strength by making him weak. I don't think this is what Jacob was expecting.

My understanding of strength… and of weakness… changed when I stood with Jacob beside the brook that night. Jacob marveled years before at Bethel that he had seen God face to face and lived to tell about it. That was years ago. Now he did more than see God. He had wrestled with him. He had rolled in the dirt with him. God would not reciprocate when Jacob asked what his name was. I don't think he needed to know any more than he already did. You are the God who blesses by crippling, who comes all the way down to the dirt with me, who will wrestle with me all night. You are the God who lets me grab hold of you, who lets me sweat and writhe in a night's-long embrace with you. You are the God who does not despise my weakness… or my strength.

When I reflected on Jacob-now-Israel I saw him walking into the Promised Land. Walking is the right metaphor. You cannot hop all the way to heaven. And you cannot run that far or for that long. You have to walk. And walking is on two legs. Jacob – and I – walk by putting one foot in front of the other. One leg swings forward, the foot comes down, and inwardly I am thinking, *"I can do all things through Christ who strengthens me."*[33] I am Israel who prevails with God and man. That's good. That's right. Now keep walking. And the other leg swings forward and the other foot comes down and a piercing pain pulses through my body, radiating from my dislocated hip. And inwardly I am thinking, "I am Jacob. I am a sinner saved and blessed by grace. I am weak and unable to prevail." Yes, you are a new creature; you are Israel. But Jacob is still there and necessarily so. That alternating rhythm between two legs is the only safe and truly blessed way to walk.

The truth is not in either foot. The truth is in the rhythm. The

[33] Philippians 4:13 The verses just before this one tell how Paul learned to be both rich and poor, abased and lifted up. That is an echo of Jacob walking on two opposed yet complimentary legs.

truth is in the living, in the walking. The thing about walking is that you never take two steps in a row on the same foot. As your confidence rises and approaches the border of pride and presumption the other foot comes down, the one connected to the dislocated hip. Sinner, weak and crippled, broken in the center of my strength. And as you begin to approach the swamp of discouragement, of fight-less defeat and cowardice thinly disguised as humility, the other foot comes down. "I can do all things… I am weak and helpless… I am Israel… I am Jacob"

There is no lack of books you can read explaining the relationship of the Old and the New man, the sin nature and the spiritual nature. Some are helpful. Some are not. Most helpful is seeing Jacob/Israel walking, seeing Jacob and his long night on the far side of Kidron. How am I going to face my Esau, my giants of temptation and fear and depression? How am I going to walk through the land that was promised but is still not yet fully mine? The answer should have long been obvious. On two legs, like Jacob. My life was saved by the story of my father Jacob/Israel. I will face Esau in the morning because I have faced God in the night and lived, and been crippled, and reborn with a new name.

"Now the sun rose upon him just as he crossed over Penuel, and he was limping on his thigh. [34]

---

[34] Genesis 32:31

SILENCE IS GOLDEN: Job's friends

When the Lamb broke the seventh seal, there was silence in heaven for about half an hour. Revelation 8:1

"Silence is golden." There is a reason why we rarely if ever hear that repeated anymore. All the evidence reveals that silence is not held in such high regard. The world is a torrent of unceasing noise. Have you pushed "scan" on your car radio lately and just let the succession of stations go by? And some of them are Christian stations.

Everyone has something to say and believes that having something to say is reason enough for saying it. There are things that should be said. But there are times, more times than we think, when silence is in order. But we fear silence. It makes us uncomfortable. We seem to believe that there is always an appropriate verse to repeat, a principle or doctrine to apply to every circumstance.

I was reading through Job. It is a very noisy book. For forty plus chapters Job's friends keep explaining Job's suffering to him. They have a well deserved very bad reputation. That is actually surprising because too many believers seem to agree with Job's friends. They are, in practice, too often examples that we emulate. "When you really have nothing to say, say something anyway" seems to be the rule that we go by. "When you have nothing to say, say nothing" would be a much better rule.

And so, given the reputation of Job's friends, I was surprised when I read of their first appearance in that most challenging of the Bible's books. It was one of those "has this always been there?—Why haven't I noticed it?—Why haven't I heard sermons and teachings on it?" moments.

> *Now when Job's three friends heard of all this adversity that had come upon him, they came each one from his own place, Eliphaz the Temanite, Bildad the Shuhite and Zophar the Naamathite; and they made an appointment together to come to sympathize with him and comfort him. When they lifted up their eyes at a distance and did not recognize him, they raised their voices and wept. And each of them tore his robe and they threw dust over their heads toward the sky. Then they sat down on the ground with him for seven days and seven nights with no one speaking a word to him, for they saw that his pain was very great.*[35]

These three men are described as friends of Job. That suggests

---

[35] Job 2:11-13

something more than a casual relationship. These are not three men who shared an hour and a half in church and an occasional potluck on Sunday with Job and his wife. They did what friends do. When they heard what was going on in Job's life; they gathered together, "*each from his own place.*" They voluntarily "displaced" themselves, left home and traveled, we don't know how far, to go see their friend. The scripture says they went "*to sympathize with him and comfort him.*" What moved them was not having and wanting to deliver "a word" for Job. Their motivation was much simpler, much more human, and therefore very spiritual. They didn't know what they would say. Job was their friend. That's all. That's a lot.

I'm not a Quaker. But I really like their official name. "The Society of Friends." I think that is a perfect name for the Church. It is a very high calling. What would the Church in the world look like and sound like; how would it appear to the world around it if it was truly a society of friends?

These three men reached a place close enough to Job's home to see him in the distance. And at their first sight of him they stopped… and they wept. Job, when God finally comes to him, says, "I have heard of you by the hearing of the ear; but now my eye sees you; therefore I retract, and I repent in dust and ashes." [36] Job's friends had heard about Job's adversity with their ears. They doubtless had talked about it among themselves as they journeyed. But now they saw him with their eyes and they stopped talking and began to weep.

---

[36] Job 42:5-6

They went from hearing to seeing. When that happens the stream of words dries up. When you see you are silent. When you see, really see the agony and suffering of your friend, all theology gets put on hold and you begin to weep. They walked on, and though the scripture does not explicitly say so I am certain they walked the rest of the way in silence.

When they reached Job "...*they sat down on the ground with him for seven days and seven nights with no one speaking a word to him, for they saw that his pain was very great.*"

I had heard those words with the hearing of the ear, but I didn't remember them. I was never arrested by them. They never shut my mouth and never made me weep. I remembered only what followed after those seven days. I remembered how those three friends could not keep from talking, how they could not keep from explaining what they could not understand, how they had to share all of their biblical knowledge and principles with Job. And what they shared was biblically sound. The principles were biblical. They just happened not be true this time.

Poor Job. I believe that his greatest torment, his greatest suffering, was not the boils he scraped with pieces of broken pottery sitting on his ash heap. The greater agony was listening to his friends explaining the inexplicable to him. And the pain of that hearing was magnified by the now lost comfort that had come to him through their silence. And I had to reflect on how much like those three friends we are, and how unlike them we are. How many times have I had the "right," the "true" biblical principles and been quick to speak them to someone sitting on his ash heap scraping his boils? But we are sadly unlike them. The truth is those three maligned, castigated friends did far better than most (then all?) of us. They sat beside their friend for seven days and seven nights and did not speak one word. We think we have been patient if we keep silent for seven minutes. They did far better, were more true, were better friends, were better representatives of God and conveyors of the comfort of the Comforter than most Christians are. We fail because we aren't truly being one another's friends. Sadly we come to each other first as "ministers" or counselors.

We know more and we know better than Job's friends, which should make us better friends. We have more knowledge and more scriptural truth. And ironically that makes it harder, almost impossible for us to sit down on the ash heaps for seven days without saying a word.

Job has saved my life by what he said later. But before that his friends, rightly reproved later by God, saved my life by what they did not say. At least as far as chapter two they taught me that I don't have to have the answers, the explanations for the adversity and agony of my fellow believers... or of myself. If I do have what I believe is the explanation, with great fear and trembling, and only after sitting in silence, I will speak it. But when I have nothing to say I have the example of those three men to encourage me to keep my heart open and my mouth shut. Silence is not empty and void. It is something to listen to, to pay attention to. It is golden.

THE PATIENCE OF JOB

We count those blessed who endured. You have heard of the endurance [patience] of Job and have seen the outcome of the Lord's dealings, that the Lord is full of compassion and is merciful. James 5:11

There is a song we used to sing when I lived in a Christian community in northern Minnesota. It began: "O Lord I want to be just like your servant Job..." I always had a hard time singing along. I don't want to be like Job. I don't want to bury all of my children in the backyard and have my health and all my possessions destroyed. And I found Job's celebrated response to his devastation inhuman, unbelievable and repellant. And yet James, in the New Testament, lifted Job up as exemplary in his patience and endurance. Something was wrong, either in me or in the song we were singing.

The song was derived from just a few verses near the beginning of Job's story. Before the second chapter of this long book is over Job is already sitting on an ash heap scraping his boils. Ever had one boil? They are very painful. Job had many of them all over his body.

His wife, witnessing the extreme suffering of her husband, comes out to him and says: *"Do you still hold fast your integrity? Curse God and die!"*[37] I understood that. Neither Job nor his wife had been informed of what took place back in chapter one. God had brought Job to the attention of Satan. And God gave Satan permission to ravage Job in order to demonstrate that Job's faithfulness and righteousness was not dependent on God's blessing and protection. When I think about it, maybe it was better that Job did not overhear that conversation in heaven. If I were Job hearing that would not have helped but would probably have made my suffering harder to bear. Job responds to his wife: *"You speak as one of the foolish women speaks. Shall we indeed accept good from God and not accept adversity?" In all this Job did not sin with his lips.*[38]

Ah, I get the message. If we accept good from the hand of God we lose all right to NOT ACCEPT adversity. Alright, but Job, this much adversity? You said that in chapter two when you had no idea how much worse it was going to get or for how long it would continue. You said that before your friends broke their silence. Without explanation? Job, you are about to get a torrent of explanations, none of which apply. Your patience is admirable, especially because you knew (and God agreed) that you are righteous. You are setting the standard rather high, Job, not just for yourself but for me. And the verse concludes, *"In all this Job did not sin with his lips."*

---

[37] Job 2:9
[38] Job 2:10

He never complained, never objected, never questioned, all the way to the end of chapter two. This raised a question for me. *"In all this Job did not sin with his lips."* "All this..." referred to what? This is only the second chapter. There is a long way to go. A lot of words are yet to be spoken by Job. Did *"In all this Job did not sin with his lips?"* apply as well to all the words he spoke AFTER chapter two? That became a very important question for me. My whole understanding of patience and endurance and faith and of God depended on the answer. Because I derived no comfort from chapter two. I did not trust Job. I did not believe him. I did not believe that the kind and degree of adversity Job suffered could indefinitely be endured without question and objection, especially when given no explanation. What saved my life was not what Job said to his wife. It is what he said, presumably without sinning, *afterwards*, that saved my trust and faith and life. He spoke a lot of words. We owe it to him and to ourselves to hear all of them.

> *Afterward Job opened his mouth and cursed the day of his birth.*
> *And Job said, let the day perish on which I was to be born, and the*
> *night which said, 'A boy is conceived. May that day be darkness; let*
> *not God above care for it, Nor light shine on it. Let darkness and*
> *black gloom claim it; let a cloud settle on it; Let the blackness of the*
> *day terrify it. As for that night, let darkness seize it; Let it not*
> *rejoice among the days of the year; let it not come into the number of*
> *the months. Behold, let that night be barren; let no joyful shout enter*
> *it. Let those curse it who curse the day, Who are prepared to rouse*
> *Leviathan. Let the stars of its twilight be darkened; let it wait for*

light but have none, And let it not see the breaking dawn; because it did not shut the opening of my mother's womb, Or hide trouble from my eyes. Why did I not die at birth, Come forth from the womb and expire? Why did the knees receive me, And why the breasts, that I should suck?

For now I would have lain down and been quiet; I would have slept then, I would have been at rest, with kings and with counselors of the earth, Who rebuilt ruins for themselves; or with princes who had gold, Who were filling their houses with silver. Or like a miscarriage which is discarded, I would not be, As infants that never saw light. There the wicked cease from raging, And there the weary are at rest. The prisoners are at ease together; They do not hear the voice of the taskmaster. The small and the great are there, and the slave is free from his master.

Why is light given to him who suffers, And life to the bitter of soul, who long for death, but there is none, and dig for it more than for hidden treasures, who rejoice greatly, and exult when they find the grave? Why is light given to a man whose way is hidden, and whom God has hedged in? [39]

"*Afterward...*" How much longer after his response to his wife did Job open his mouth and pour out these words? How long do you have to sit on your ash heap scraping your boils before all sweet piety and patience is swept away and all you can wish is that you had been a miscarriage, that you had never been born? Now I can listen to Job.

---

[39] Job 3:1-23

Now I can take him as an example of patience and endurance. Now my understanding of patience is incarnated, is explained in a life of real flesh and blood, and a response to suffering and desolation that I can understand. Now Job is no longer a paper saint in a holy book stripped of all credible humanity. I found it impossibly hard to hear myself speaking like Job in chapter two. I found it all too easy to hear his words in chapter three coming out of my mouth. And now I was beginning to understand how he endured all those chapters between three and the end of the book. Suffering makes you not only patient; it makes you true; it makes you honest; it makes you real. Patience is the prerogative of the real and true.

When God finally steps on the stage and addresses Job it is with great power. But it is without anger, without a word about any of Job's words in chapter three, or any of the succeeding chapters. And so I have concluded that *"In all this Job did not sin with his lips"* applies to both chapter two and chapter three, and all the chapters to the end of the book. And that has saved my life and my faith. It can be taken wrongly. Just about everything can. It can be taken as license to rail at and blame God, to wallow in the deeps of self-pity and self-justification. That is not what Job did. That is not what I want permission to do. Job gave an honest report, an honest description of the state of his soul. "I want to be just like your servant Job" not only in his untested sentiments in chapter two. I want to be like Job in his utterly honest and believable humanity. I want to be like Job in the shocking freedom, which is to say, faith, with which he bared his heart, his whole heart, his stretched-beyond-breaking human heart before God. What is it that Jesus said was the greatest commandment? Love the Lord with your whole heart and mind and soul and strength. How can you do that when you have pre-censored some of your deepest, truest thoughts and emotions? With half your heart you can only love half of God. I believe God rejoices when the partitions in our minds and hearts crumble and fall, when our hearts are united, whole. (*Teach me Your way, O LORD; I will walk in Your truth; Unite my heart to fear Your name.*[40])

He waits for the whole of us to seek the whole of him. When I read scripture what stands out more than anything else is that God does not make only a part of himself known. Does he expect me to expose only part of myself to him? I am not looking for a God who will excuse my sin. I am looking for a God who is looking for honest men and women with undivided hearts.

In the end Job repented. I am beginning to understand what it was he repented of. God finally comes to Job and at considerable length proclaims his unimaginable greatness as the creator of all things. And then, in chapter forty he interjects in the midst of the catalog of his great creative works, these words: "6 Then the LORD answered Job out of the storm and said,

Now gird up your loins like a man; I will ask you, and you instruct Me. Will you really annul My judgment? Will you condemn Me that you may be justified? Or do you have an arm like God, And can you thunder with a voice like His? Adorn yourself with eminence and

---

[40] Psalm 86:11

dignity, And clothe yourself with honor and majesty. Pour out the overflowings of your anger, And look on everyone who is proud, and make him low. Look on everyone who is proud, and humble him, And tread down the wicked where they stand. Hide them in the dust together; Bind them in the hidden place. Then I will also confess to you, that your own right hand can save you.[41]

I had fully identified with Job. I had asked for (or had I demanded?) an explanation from God. And As I stood beside Job I took up what I felt was our joint complaint: "God, you haven't answered me!" Where is the explanation for all this suffering? You aren't even telling Job about the conversation in heaven in chapter one. And I listened as God gave what to his mind was all the explanation required. And summed up it came to this: "Job, I am God. And you are not." It was when God challenged Job and asked him, not only, "Where were you when I hung the galaxies?" but when he said *"Look on everyone who is proud, and humble him, And tread down the wicked where they stand. Hide them in the dust together; Bind them in the hidden place."*

I can't do that. But that was just the prelude to the last and decisive point. Humble the proud and ***"Then I will also confess to you, that your own right hand can save yourself."*** Save myself? Where did that come from? Is that what all of my arguing and challenging God amounted to? Is that the heart of what Job repented of? I cannot save myself. Case closed.

---

[41] Job 40:7-14

"I have heard of You by the hearing of the ear; But now my eye sees You; therefore I retract, and I repent in dust and ashes."[42] I had been living by what I had heard as if I had seen it. I repented of resting in my pursuit of truth and God with what I had only heard and not come to see. Seeing God answers all questions. Seeing God settles all disputes. "I cannot save myself" silences all of my objections.

And then God addresses the three friends who began so well but who had to open their mouths and had to speak about God to Job.

> *It came about after the LORD had spoken these words to Job, that the LORD said to Eliphaz the Temanite, "My wrath is kindled against you and against your two friends, because you have not spoken of Me what is right as My servant Job has.*[43]

The "correct" words of Job's friends kindled the wrath of God. The "biblically correct" words of these three religious church attendees kindled THE WRATH OF GOD.

God's anger is for the very religious, very "biblical," very "righteous" friends who, having never suffered like Job, having never been perplexed and overwhelmed by the inexplicable turning of their lives, presumed to explain to the man on the ash heap who God was and what God was doing. Now it is not Job but God himself telling them they are the ones who have sinned with their mouths; they are

---

[42] Job 42:5-6
[43] Job 42:7

the ones who have misrepresented God and that it is Job who has spoken what is right. So, Job did not sin with any of the words of his lips. His three friends had. Underlying all of their confident, principled, "biblical" answers was the belief that they could save themselves.

Lord, I want to be just like your servant Job. I want to speak what is right, what is true about you. I want to see you as you really are and not merely as I have heard with the hearing of my ears. Like Job, I want to be able to pray for my friends.

A WHITE STONE, HIDDEN MANNA:
REVELATION 2:17

There are a number of rewards for overcoming, or persevering, mentioned in the Revelation. Among them is this one: *To him who overcomes, to him I will give some of the hidden manna, and I will give him a white stone, and a new name written on the stone which no one knows but he who receives it.'* [44] Along with ruling over cities and sitting on the throne beside the Lord there is the promise of some of the hidden manna. He is the bread of life given to every believer. So what is this "hidden manna" and why is it hidden? And with the hidden manna is a white stone with a name written on it, a name that is unique, that is quintessentially personal; a name that is known only to the one who receives it and to the one who gives it.

A reward is an encouragement to keep going, to endure. It has to be something desirable, otherwise it is not a reward, not a motivation. So why should receiving hidden manna and a white stone with a new

---

[44] Revelation 2:17

name that only I and the Lord know be an encouragement?

I'm not sure I understand all that "hidden manna" means. But I know it implies something unique, something "private" and intimate. This is not bread laid out in the middle of the table for everyone to share. It is not out in open view of everyone. The one who made this bread made it for one person sitting at the table and hid it from everyone else. And with it is a white stone with that person's name on it, a name that no one else shares. Wasn't it a hallmark of the newborn church in Jerusalem that no one considered anything simply his own but they held all things in common?[45] Yes, they shared their possessions. They shared the bread on the family table. But this is not that bread; this is hidden manna. They shared a common family name, one spirit, one divine paternity. But the name on the white stone is not the family name; it is the given name, given by one who alone knows your true name, the one who gives it to you and you alone. No one else knows it. No one else can know it because no one else knows you perfectly, truly, as you really are.

This white stone is a reward for overcoming. Okay; overcoming what? I had been taught that it was self that I had to overcome. "Die to self," "put the old man/self to death," "hate even your own life..." True. But what does it mean? At times it sounded a lot like what my old Hindu and Buddhist teachers meant: the complete elimination of self. But if that's what it meant, who is the "me" in whom Christ lives? My first theological question as a new believer of

---

[45] Acts 2:42-45

several weeks arose when I was reading Paul's letter to the Galatians. Paul wrote that it is no longer I who live but Christ who lives in me.[46] So, if it is no longer I who live, who is the me? There is still a me. I don't disappear. The "me" isn't absorbed into God like a drop of water in the ocean. There is still someone there whose name is written on that white stone. What became clear was that it was sin, it was everything that bent and warped and perverted my desires and appetites and my whole personality that had to be overcome. Overcoming was my part to play, not in obliterating my self but in setting self, my personality, free. Salvation was not the destruction of self; it was the process liberating, of finally becoming myself. *"Whom the Son sets free is free indeed."*[47] Yes! I didn't long to be erased; I longed to be set free. Overcoming gluttony doesn't destroy appetite, it sets it free.

There was no question of opting for "cheap grace." I wasn't looking for an excuse to indulge every impulse and desire of my mind and body. But my body (and my mind) was not my enemy. Saint Francis called his body "brother ass." It was a stubborn mule that sometimes had to be kicked and prodded to go where I wanted it to go. It was an ass, but it was my brother. And I am my brother's keeper. And there was the resurrection of the body to look forward to. Like Paul the apostle I wasn't longing to finally be set free from the body. I wanted it to be transformed, not done away with. I wanted it to do what it was originally meant to do, created to do: to

---

[46] Galatians 2:20
[47] John 8:36

perfectly express all that caused God to say when he had breathed life into it, "Very good." The body was home to all the appetites and desires that served sin. But the appetites were not evil; sin had bent them. God was all about getting them unbent.

And it was the body that grounded our individuality. Believers, said Paul the apostle, are "one body in Christ." But that didn't' make us all the same. The stomach was united with all the other organs beneath my skin, but it never stopped being very distinct, it never lost its identity, its stomach-ness. And it's a good thing it didn't. The body works because all of its parts remain themselves. So I was left wondering just what was my identity as a believing Christian. How did God feel about my "personality," my uniqueness?

God's first commandment to man was to multiply. He didn't clone Adam. He didn't make him to multiply like an amoeba, producing exact duplicates of himself. God apparently wasn't after a choir that would sing only in unison. He wanted something much better. He wanted harmony. Unison can be good. But harmony is "very good."

So the reward for overcoming is not the obliteration of self, not absorption into some selfless state. As important and satisfying as the corporate aspect of salvation is, as great as being a part or member of something much bigger than myself, called the Church, or the Body of Christ, is, that does not diminish or eclipse the very individual and unique aspect of knowing and being known by God. In fact, eternal individuality is an essential, an indispensable condition for being part of a greater whole. The reward for overcoming self is becoming truly, freely, eternally oneself.

There is a natural and frankly very understandable resistance among some Christians, as well as in most religions, to individuality. It is suspected of being the refuge of egotism and selfishness, of inflated self-importance. But though it can be that, it is not necessarily that. And an extreme emphasis on the corporate side of life is no less contrary to God's design than rampant individualism. It has its own dangers. It can and often does reduce all expressions of individual uniqueness and personality and difference to an anonymous, homogenized blob.

In the old myth, Procrustus had a guest who spent the night at his house. But there was a problem. His bed was too short for his guest. He solved the problem by cutting off his guest's feet. The bed was no longer too short. That was not the best solution. That is not God's solution.

We are one body together. But the body lives and works because all of its different parts do not lose their individual identities. It lives and works because each part retains its individuality. The foot has no reason to envy or resent the eye. And neither does the eye have to apologize for seeing and being all the way up near the top of the head. It would not be humility for the eye to hold its eyelid tightly shut in order to not offend or make the foot jealous. The eye has one ultimate calling and purpose: to be the best eye it can be, to see and to delight in seeing. And when it does THAT it should make not just itself, but the foot very glad.

I had for years heard "self" being condemned and berated as if having a unique, individual personality was the same as self-centered egotism. I struggled long and hard with what I was hearing and being taught, until I read and really heard, *"I will give him a white stone, and a new name written on the stone which no one knows but he who receives it."*

The God of the Bible is three persons in the most perfect unity yet without in the slightest degree diminishing the uniqueness and personality of each person. The New Testament is one consistent word. But John still sounds like John and Luke like Luke and Paul very much like Paul. So if that is the very nature of God and of his word, what must become of us when we overcome all that separates us from him and from each other? My destiny is be conformed to the likeness of the Son of God, not to become his clone or carbon copy. I am unique. I don't know if no two snowflakes are ever exactly alike. I do know that no two people are ever exactly alike, not even identical twins.

Then I understood the biblical view of self. Selflessness is not the absence of self. It is the freedom to delight in, to enjoy and encourage selves other than my own, no less than I delight in the gracious miracle and wonder of being, like God himself, a person, a someone, a self. Now I understand that being a unique self in not an obstacle to love. It is a precondition for love. God is love and he is the original Self. He is totally and perfectly himself. And that is what he means for us be.

"Therefore you are to be perfect, as your heavenly Father is perfect." Matthew 5:48

I have been stunned at times while reading and coming to a perfect sentence or a perfect image. It expresses something completely, and beautifully. And it is a source of great delight and joy. A perfect meal, or conversation, or baseball game, or whatever, has that effect. You have just experienced something as it was always meant to be. You can never be fully satisfied with less again. If you are a violinist you keep trading up for a better violin. It is not greed or selfishness to do so. You hear the music in your head. And you want the best instrument possible so that what you hear in your head can come out of your head and fill the room. And be heard and delighted in by others. That is not selfishness. It is love. It is why God in the beginning created the heavens and the earth. And us.

A quartet, or a symphony orchestra, is the coming together and playing together of many soloists. Unity is a function of a number of ones coming together. (Every number, however big, is a collection of a lot of ones.) They become something far greater than the sum of their parts not because they cease to be soloists, but because when they come together they remain and become all the more truly themselves.

JOY: HEBREWS 12

... fixing our eyes on Jesus, the author and perfecter of faith, who for the joy set before Him endured the cross, despising the shame, and has sat down at the right hand of the throne of God. *Hebrews 12:2*

In the eighteenth century a German philosopher named Immanuel Kant said that for an act to be virtuous or praiseworthy it had to be completely devoid of any self interest. If my act gave me any benefit or pleasure it was thereby tainted. The moral value of an act depended entirely on the motive behind it. It had to be selfless to be good. That understanding has permeated religious and Christian thinking and gone largely unquestioned. It is assumed by many that Kant's understanding is what the Bible also teaches. I assumed it as a new follower of Jesus. After all, isn't that what makes Jesus perfect and sinless? Didn't he do everything in obedience to his father, in total disregard of all self-interest and benefit? And he was only doing what he saw his father doing – like father like son. So he was motivated by duty alone, which meant he did nothing for his own pleasure and benefit.

But when I thought about it, it led to some disturbing conclusions. For one, it implied a very dismal, repellant view of God. Since God was perfectly good he did nothing out of a wrong motive. That meant he derived no pleasure from creating the universe, or being good, or showing mercy. I really didn't want to be around a God like that, certainly not forever. I didn't want to be around any people like that either. They think loving and liking, or enjoying something are completely unrelated. Actually they think that as soon as you start liking something your loving it becomes tainted. So, the best chef doesn't enjoy cooking? And he doesn't enjoy the food he cooks? So, the people who like me the least love me the most? So, the truest love is devoid of all liking and enjoying? So, God, who is love, doesn't like or enjoy me, or himself, or anything at all?

I was very troubled by this understanding of love and of righteousness. I wondered, what did God have in mind when he commanded me to love him? And what was Paul intending when he said that the Kingdom of God wasn't eating and drinking but righteousness, peace and joy?[48] Righteousness? Of course; indisputable. Peace? Yes. But joy? Paul seemed to be saying that joy was an equal partner with righteousness and peace, an indispensable

---

[48] Romans 14:17

partner. It turns out that, despite sounding very religious and spiritual, Kant's view is not at all biblical.

There were plenty of people in church quick to point out that Jesus said that whoever seeks to save his life will lose it, that unless you hated your own life you couldn't be his disciple. Pleasure was highly suspect. I understood that. But something was not right. What seemed to follow was that Heaven was a very serious place, much like a church service where everyone sat on a hard pew and all the men wore slightly too tight shirts with the top button buttoned and ties pulled up tight. Heaven was like that kind of church service, except it never ended. Heaven, where God lived, must be joyless, which I supposed was better than a place of constant suffering and pain, but not by much.

Intuitively I sensed that joy was not a take-it-or-leave-it sort of thing. It wasn't the nice but completely unnecessary icing on the cake of salvation. I sensed it was part of the cake, something to be pursued, not just as a possible effect of righteousness but as intrinsically bound up in righteousness. Yes, Jesus said that he who seeks to save his life will lose it. But he went on to say that he who loses his life for Jesus' sake will gain it. He who loses this passing life will gain eternal life. He was saying give up a present joy for the sake of attaining a greater one.

Then I was invited to come and hear someone speaking to a

large assembly of Christian pastors and leaders. He spoke about motivating Christian believers to radical obedience, to self-denial, to "death to self." But how he believed people are best motivated to "radical obedience" was not something I had ever heard before.

He spoke about the first few verses of chapter twelve of Hebrews. It turned my understanding upside down; it rearranged everything, like someone turning a kaleidoscope one hundred and eighty degrees in one sudden twist. All the little colored stones were still there. None were added or taken away. But when they landed they made a totally different picture.

If we were reading the original manuscript of the letter to the Hebrews there would be no division between chapters eleven and twelve. Hebrews chapter eleven is rightly known as the faith chapter in the Bible. The chapter is built around examples of people acting in faith. It focuses on their motives. *"By faith Abraham, when he was called, obeyed by going out to a place which he was to receive for an inheritance; and he went out, not knowing where he was going."*[49] This is the faith that pleases God. Nothing but faith pleases God. Abraham went *not knowing*. I thought he must have read a pre-publication copy of Immanuel Kant. Faith must be blind, raw obedience to be praiseworthy, right? Faith is contrary to sight, right? I was told so. I thought so. Until the day I heard what the Bible was actually saying.

---

[49] Hebrews 11:8

Two verses later we are told that Abraham was looking for something. *"...For he was looking for the city which has foundations, whose architect and builder is God."* (11:10) I know why I look for something. It's because I want to find it, because I desire it. Because I value it. And I must have some idea or picture of what it looks like. How else would I recognize it when I found it?

> *All these died in faith, without receiving the promises, but having seen them and having welcomed them from a distance, and having confessed that they were strangers and exiles on the earth. For those who say such things make it clear that they are seeking a country of their own. And indeed if they had been thinking of that country from which they went out, they would have had opportunity to return. But as it is, they desire a better country, that is, a heavenly one. Therefore God is not ashamed to be called their God; for He has prepared a city for them.*[50]

"All these" includes Abraham. So Abraham *saw something*. He saw it in the distance and welcomed it. When he saw it he opened his heart to it and it took hold of his affections. He desired it. It was pleasing to him, desirable to him. That's why he packed his bags and left all the comforts of what had been home. He *"DESIRED a better country."* That disqualified him in Immanuel Kant's eyes. And it is precisely what qualified him in God's sight. *"THEREFORE God is not ashamed to be called their God; for He has prepared a city for them"*

If you keep reading you get to Moses living in Pharoah's palace. He left all that wealth and privilege. Why? What motivated him?

---

[50] Hebrews 11:13-16

By faith Moses, when he had grown up, refused to be called the son of Pharaoh's daughter, choosing rather to endure ill-treatment with the people of God than to enjoy the passing pleasures of sin, considering the reproach of Christ greater riches than the treasures of Egypt; for he was looking to the reward. By faith he left Egypt, not fearing the wrath of the king; for he endured, as seeing Him who is unseen.[51]

This was not dispassionate, raw obedience. Moses, like Abraham, saw something, something that was better than all the comforts and pleasures of Egypt. He desired and valued it more and so he left Egypt behind. But the example greater than Abraham and Moses is in the beginning of chapter twelve.

Therefore, since we have so great a cloud of witnesses surrounding us, let us also lay aside every encumbrance and the sin which so easily entangles us, and let us run with endurance the race that is set before us, fixing our eyes on Jesus, the author and perfecter of faith, who for the joy set before Him endured the cross, despising the shame, and has sat down at the right hand of the throne of God. For consider Him who has endured such hostility by sinners against Himself, so that you will not grow weary and lose heart.[52]

"*... for the joy set before him...*" Jesus saw something. The writer doesn't tell us what it was that he saw. What we are told is that it was a great joy, it was something so redolent with delight, so desirable that it made all the suffering and anguish of crucifixion worth

---

[51] Hebrews 11:24-27
[52] Hebrews 12: 1-3

enduring. He was motivated by the joy set before him. The writer could have said that submission and obedience to his father was what moved him to endure crucifixion. And that would be true but liable to be misleading, unless you recall David saying, "*Sacrifice and meal offering You have not desired; My ears You have opened; Burnt offering and sin offering You have not required. Then I said, "Behold, I come; In the scroll of the book it is written of me. I delight to do Your will, O my God; Your Law is within my heart."*[53] I DELIGHT to do your will? What would Kant have to say to David, or to Jesus?

Did Jesus need something more than the prospect of obeying and pleasing his Father to enable him to endure the suffering and shame? That's the wrong question. It was not something more, it was something intrinsically bound up in surrender to his Father's will. The great joy set before him was part, an essential part, of his Father's will. It was his Father who set it before him. As he sets it before us.

Some Christians seem to think they need to be more spiritual than Jesus, the Son of God. Jesus may have needed a great joy to motivate him but we don't. Obedience is its own reward. We don't need some pleasure or delight to get us to do what is right. That sounds very spiritual. Actually it doesn't when you think about it. Does my pleasure in making you happy detract from or increase the virtue of what I do? Enjoying doing what is righteous, what is loving, doesn't make me less like God; it makes me more like him. Did God

---

[53] Psalm 40:6-8

make a mistake when he told us there were rewards waiting for us in heaven?

When I saw that Jesus was moved by the prospect of a great joy it set something free in me. It set me free to be human. Not to go running after every natural pleasure and indulge myself. It gave me a reason and a new strength to do just the opposite, to turn my back on lesser, distracting pleasures in order to pursue a greater, more lasting, more satisfying one. That's what Abraham did. That's what Moses did. That's what Jesus did. Those are good examples to follow.

HELP MY UNBLELIEF: MARK 9:24

Faith is, to say the obvious, important, very important, critically important. It is impossible to please God without it.[54] We are justified by faith alone. So how I understand faith and how it works and how God relates to it is crucial. I have been perplexed by what I find said in scripture about faith and even more confused by what I have heard said about faith by fellow believers over my years as a follower of Jesus. "Ask and it will be given to you... When two or more of you agree about ANYTHING..." What exactly does that mean? How about "If you have faith the size of a mustard seed you can command a mountain to be removed and it will be." Jesus said that. He quantified faith, or rather, he de-quantified it. He said that it is not a matter of how much faith you have. A little faith, a very little, goes a long way. I have only rarely felt like I had a lot of faith, though how one measures faith, how I would know how much faith I had, is not at all obvious to me. I do know that whatever quantity of faith I might have had, I have never spoken to a mountain and seen it moved.

---

[54] Hebrews 11:6

So it was comforting to find that I was not alone in my confusion. The twelve disciples, the inner circle of Jesus' chosen apostles, shared my perplexity. A man came to Jesus seeking mercy, asking him to heal his son.

> *When they came to the crowd, a man came up to Jesus, falling on his knees before Him and saying, "Lord, have mercy on my son, for he is a lunatic and is very ill; for he often falls into the fire and often into the water. Then he added, "I brought him to your disciples, and they could not cure him."*[55]

I have always found Jesus response more than a little shocking and disturbing, and at the same time strangely comforting. *"And Jesus answered and said, "You unbelieving and perverted generation, how long shall I be with you? Bring him here to Me."*[56] Matthew doesn't specify to whom Jesus was responding. Was he speaking to his disciples? Or to the sick boy's father? Or both? *"Unbelieving and perverted generation…"* That is a very strong characterization. And then Matthew records Jesus saying, *"How long shall I put up with you?"*

I took that very personally. Is that how you feel about me? About all of us? Is that how you feel about your disciples when they lack the faith to command a demonic spirit to release a young boy? Is that what you feel about my unbelief when I can't command a mountain to move out of the way? If I were Matthew I don't think I would have written that into my report. And at the same time I was thankful

---

[55] Mathew 17:14-16
[56] Matthew 17:17

for the surprising candor of what Matthew chose to include. It was another glimpse into the real human emotion and responses of the man Jesus of Nazareth, another life-saving bit of scripture, another evidence of the reality and meaning of incarnation.

And Jesus rebuked him, and the demon came out of him, and the boy was cured at once. Then the disciples came to Jesus privately and said, "Why could we not drive it out?" And He said to them, "Because of the littleness of your faith; for truly I say to you, if you have faith the size of a mustard seed, you will say to this mountain, 'Move from here to there,' and it will move; and nothing will be impossible to you." [57]

The disciples asked Jesus the right question. It has been my question for a long, long time. And I think if we are all honest we would all acknowledge having that same question in mind. Jesus' answer has not been very comforting to me. He said that this mountain in front of me was not removed because I lacked the requisite faith, which is faith the size of a mustard seed. But, when disturbed or confused, the solution seems often, if not always, just a few verses away.

Mark relates the same incident but with an important additional detail.

They brought the boy to Him. When he saw Him, immediately the spirit threw him into a convulsion, and falling to the ground, he began

---

[57] Matthew 17:18-19

rolling around and foaming at the mouth. And He asked his father, "How long has this been happening to him?" And he said, "From childhood. It has often thrown him both into the fire and into the water to destroy him. But if you can do anything, take pity on us and help us!" And Jesus said to him, "'If you can?' All things are possible to him who believes." Immediately the boy's father cried out and said, "I do believe; help my unbelief."[58]

Mark's account is more graphic than Matthew's. Mark's mountain is in fuller view and it is big, very big. A desperate, loving father, the incarnate Son of God, and his chosen disciples along with an unspecified number of onlookers are watching a young boy convulsing, rolling on the ground, foaming at the mouth. Jesus asks the boy's father how long this has been happening and the father says, from childhood. He has been living with this mountain before him for many years. And the father then says, *"if you can do anything, take pity on us and help us!"*

And Jesus said to him, *"'If you can?' All things are possible to him who believes."* Jesus, and now Mark, leave us with no doubt that he heard and understood the "if." It is not the word you say when you are certain. Does this man not know who he is talking to? He is asking the one through whom God spoke the universe into existence. This desperate father is less than certain. Is this faith? Jesus responds, *"All things are possible to him who believes."* Who believes? Jesus is certain. Jesus knows that he can do this. The boy's father is not certain; he is

---

[58] Mark 9:20-24

only desperate.

He responds: *"I do believe; help my unbelief."* This is what I was waiting for a long time to hear. This is what made the whole incident life-saving and faith-saving for me. It is too tempting to dismiss and explain away this troubled man as having no faith. Can faith and uncertainty both be present at the same time? There is application often made of this passage of Scripture that puts the focus on the disciples, on us as the one's called upon to exercise faith as the bearers of healing and deliverance. I know that Jesus says *"this one comes out only by prayer."* Some manuscripts add *"and fasting."* I am content to let others debate which manuscripts are more accurate and exactly what *"with prayer and fasting"* means here. But when I was drawn into the incident I found myself standing beside the desperate father, not the disciples. Was Jesus saying to me that if I had faith like a mustard seed I would not be saying "if" to him? But the father did have faith. *"I believe,"* he said.

And that is why this father's answer has meant so much to me. Standing face to face with Jesus he says, *"I believe."* Really? Jesus did not shoot down that response. He didn't tell him he was obviously wrong, that he clearly DID NOT BELIEVE! He did believe. And because he did believe he said, *"Help my unbelief!"* I was stunned by his response. He was saying that belief could, and often, perhaps always, does exist right alongside unbelief. I could relate to that. I knew what he was saying. I understood immediately what he was saying. Lord, help my unbelief. I had never heard that before. I had felt it; I had wanted to say it. And now I could say it because I heard this anguished father say it to Jesus. And Jesus did not correct or reprove him. Jesus didn't say, "Unbelief! Why don't you go home and come back when you have rid yourself of all of your unbelief. Go home and pray and fast. Come back when you believe fully and then maybe I will heal your son." No, this father had belief, about the size of a mustard seed. And all around it was unbelief.

I have long seen faith as an island surrounded by a sea of doubt. Like the tide of the sea, unbelief comes in and goes out. Sometimes there is a high tide when the water covers the beach and most of the island. Sometimes there is only enough dry land above water to plant your two feet on. But the water stops rising. Faith, down to the size of a mustard seed, is not extinguished. And at times the tide goes out, out very far. The beach reappears. The island seems very, very large, as large as a continent. And it is then that we forget that even a continent, every continent, is really just a very big island.

I'm not looking for an excuse for unbelief and doubt. I am looking for an honest account of what the life of faith is really like. I am looking for an honest picture of the human soul in which faith stands beside unbelief and asks for help. I am looking for a realistic, incarnate understanding and experience of belief that I can bring to someone struggling with what faith means, who is not being helped by all the mindless exhortations to "just believe!" I want something to say to someone who isn't being helped by all the rebukes for his lack of faith. I want to be able to speak truth and comforting reality

94

to myself and to others whose high, shadow-casting mountains don't just go away. We are saved by faith, and that not of ourselves. It is a gift of God.[59]

---

[59] Ephesians 2:8

THE CONCLUSION

INCARNATION: In the beginning and in the end.

The whole biblical story begins with a perfect creation and ends in resurrection and the restoration of the perfect goodness of what was there in the beginning. And from beginning to end, it seems to me, it is all about incarnation. The creation is the incarnation, the giving of a body, to the ideas in the mind of God. Every tree and star and grain of sand is the embodiment of an idea, a word, in the mind of God. The creation of man is the incarnation of the image of God in a body of earth. And the story that follows is about the ruinous breakdown of the once-good creation, most especially of man. And in the end the whole creation is brought down into death, dissolved down to the elements not so that it can be done away with but so that it can be resurrected. The final book of the Bible is about not just a new heavens but a new earth in which righteousness reigns. So incarnation is not just a necessary, temporary expedient whereby God atones for and removes sin from the world. It is the permanent condition, the beginning and the end of the whole story. God will have the perfect embodiment of all of his ideas, most especially of man. When Jesus ascended back to his father he did not leave his human body behind. He ascended with it. He still has it, and always will.

And so it should not be surprising that all along the way grace and faith and righteousness and joy should be found incarnated in the lives of real men and women. The Church, the people of God, is an ongoing incarnation. Incarnation is God's grand idea. The glory of God is not diminished by being incarnated in the body of the Son of God. It is magnified in him and in the new humanity, the people of God, the Church. It is the what and why of creation and of redemption. It will all become clear in a day that will come surprisingly soon. Having this sure hope, we persevere.

Seeing Is Believing.

Or is it, "believing is seeing"? What do we say when we have been struggling to understand something and finally we "get it"? "Ah, I see what you mean!" I have seen joy embodied in a man who passed through a long, very dark night of sorrow and grief. I have seen freedom embodied in a man who met Jesus, the Messiah, about mid way through twenty-two years in prison. And I have seen, known and received the grace of God embodied in my wife and a few true friends who themselves had come to know, at great cost, the grace they showed to me. I have seen and known faith and joy and truth incarnated in Abraham and Job and David and a desperate father.

And so now I understand what Jesus meant when he said I had to eat his flesh and drink his blood to have his life in me. Really understanding, really receiving truth, is much more like eating and drinking than drawing a logical conclusion or solving a puzzle. The life of the Son of God enters us like food and drink and breath. That's how it gets into not just our brain but every cell of our body. That's how it becomes ours. And we become his. We really are what we eat. So "eat, drink, and be merry, be filled with joy, for tomorrow... for tomorrow we live – and will live – forever on this bread and drink and joy." I believe that, now more, much more than I did when I first believed.

ABOUT THE AUTHOR

Paul Volk was born in Brooklyn, New York where he studied and taught philosophy for several years before leaving Brooklyn for California. It was there, in 1973, that he was confronted with the real Jesus of Nazareth and became his follower.

For nearly eight years he lived and worked, with his wife Adrienne, in a Christian community/ministry in northern Minnesota.

In 1992, at the age of forty-four, he received a Master's Degree in Theology from Bethel Seminary in Saint Paul.

He has traveled and taught on biblical themes in Europe, Africa, Asia and South America. After thirty-eight years in the Upper Midwest he and Adrienne moved back to Berkeley, California, where they are part of a ministry at the University of California, Berkeley, to visiting scholars and students from China

If you have gotten all the way to this page you just might be interested in reading more. There's a blog, part of a website, with a number of shorter writings. (paulvolk.org) And several more books are available on Amazon. Searching on the author's name should get you there.

If you have questions, comments, objections or just want to get in contact you can through the website or directly at paulvolk68@gmail.com

www.ingramcontent.com/pod-product-compliance
Lightning Source LLC
Chambersburg PA
CBHW031325040426
42443CB00005B/222